OPPOSING
VIEWPOINTS®
SERIES

D0372675

Hunting

Other Books of Related Interest:

Opposing Viewpoints Series

Conserving the Environment

The Environment

At Issue Series

Do Animals Have Rights?

How Should America's Wilderness Be Managed?

Managing America's Forests

Current Controversies Series

Conserving the Environment

"Congress shall make no law . . . abridging the freedom of speech, or of the press."

First Amendment to the U.S. Constitution

The basic foundation of our democracy is the First Amendment guarantee of freedom of expression. The Opposing Viewpoints series is dedicated to the concept of this basic freedom and the idea that it is more important to practice it than to enshrine it.

**OPPOSING
VIEWPOINTS®
SERIES**

Hunting

Dawn Laney, Book Editor

GREENHAVEN PRESS

An imprint of Thomson Gale, a part of The Thomson Corporation

THOMSON

™

GALE

Detroit • New York • San Francisco • New Haven, Conn. • Waterville, Maine • London

Christine Nasso, *Publisher*
Elizabeth Des Chenes, *Managing Editor*

© 2008 The Gale Group.

Star logo is a trademark and Gale and Greenhaven Press are registered trademarks used herein under license.

For more information, contact:
Greenhaven Press
27500 Drake Rd.
Farmington Hills, MI 48331-3535
Or you can visit our Internet site at http://www.gale.com

Articles in Greenhaven Press anthologies are often edited for length to meet page requirements. In addition, original titles of these works are changed to clearly present the main thesis and to explicitly indicate the author's opinion. Every effort is made to ensure that Greenhaven Press accurately reflects the original intent of the authors. Every effort has been made to trace the owners of copyrighted material.

Cover photograph reproduced by permission of photos.com.

ISBN-13: 978-0-7377-3896-4 (hardcover)
ISBN-10: 0-7377-3896-0 (hardcover)
ISBN-13: 978-0-7377-3897-1 (pbk.)
ISBN-10: 0-7377-3897-9 (pbk.)

2007938708

Contents

Chapter 3: Is Hunting an Important Part of Wildlife Maintenance?

Why Consider Opposing Viewpoints?

"The only way in which a human being can make some approach to knowing the whole of a subject is by hearing what can be said about it by persons of every variety of opinion and studying all modes in which it can be looked at by every character of mind. No wise man ever acquired his wisdom in any mode but this."

John Stuart Mill

In our media-intensive culture it is not difficult to find differing opinions. Thousands of newspapers and magazines and dozens of radio and television talk shows resound with differing points of view. The difficulty lies in deciding which opinion to agree with and which "experts" seem the most credible. The more inundated we become with differing opinions and claims, the more essential it is to hone critical reading and thinking skills to evaluate these ideas. Opposing Viewpoints books address this problem directly by presenting stimulating debates that can be used to enhance and teach these skills. The varied opinions contained in each book examine many different aspects of a single issue. While examining these conveniently edited opposing views, readers can develop critical thinking skills such as the ability to compare and contrast authors' credibility, facts, argumentation styles, use of persuasive techniques, and other stylistic tools. In short, the Opposing Viewpoints series is an ideal way to attain the higher-level thinking and reading skills so essential in a culture of diverse and contradictory opinions.

In addition to providing a tool for critical thinking, Opposing Viewpoints books challenge readers to question their own strongly held opinions and assumptions. Most people form their opinions on the basis of upbringing, peer pressure, and personal, cultural, or professional bias. By reading carefully balanced opposing views, readers must directly confront new ideas as well as the opinions of those with whom they disagree. This is not to simplistically argue that everyone who reads opposing views will—or should—change his or her opinion. Instead, the series enhances readers' understanding of their own views by encouraging confrontation with opposing ideas. Careful examination of others' views can lead to the readers' understanding of the logical inconsistencies in their own opinions, perspective on why they hold an opinion, and the consideration of the possibility that their opinion requires further evaluation.

Evaluating Other Opinions

To ensure that this type of examination occurs, Opposing Viewpoints books present all types of opinions. Prominent spokespeople on different sides of each issue as well as well-known professionals from many disciplines challenge the reader. An additional goal of the series is to provide a forum for other, less-known, or even unpopular viewpoints. The opinion of an ordinary person who has had to make the decision to cut off life support from a terminally ill relative, for example, may be just as valuable and provide just as much insight as a medical ethicist's professional opinion. The editors have two additional purposes in including these less-known views. One, the editors encourage readers to respect others' opinions—even when not enhanced by professional credibility. It is only by reading or listening to and objectively evaluating others' ideas that one can determine whether they are worthy of consideration. Two, the inclusion of such viewpoints encourages the important critical thinking skill of objectively evaluating an author's credentials and bias. This evaluation will illuminate an author's reasons for taking a particular stance on an issue and will aid in readers' evaluation of the author's ideas.

It is our hope that these books will give readers a deeper understanding of the issues debated and an appreciation of the complexity of even seemingly simple issues when good and honest people disagree. This awareness is particularly important in a democratic society such as ours in which people enter into public debate to determine the common good. Those with whom one disagrees should not be regarded as enemies but rather as people whose views deserve careful examination and may shed light on one's own.

Thomas Jefferson once said that "difference of opinion leads to inquiry, and inquiry to truth." Jefferson, a broadly educated man, argued that "if a nation expects to be ignorant and free . . . it expects what never was and never will be." As individuals and as a nation, it is imperative that we consider the opinions of others and examine them with skill and discernment. The Opposing Viewpoints series is intended to help readers achieve this goal.

David L. Bender and Bruno Leone,
Founders

Introduction

*"Our prehistoric ancestors were hunters.
To them, animals were as sacred as life
itself. A good hunt assured survival."*

The National Shooting
Sports Foundation

*"Hunting is not a sport. In a sport, both
sides should know they're in the game."*

Paul Rodriguez

Over the past one hundred years, hunting in the United
States has undergone a transformation from the necessary work of providing food and safety for families into a predominantly recreational activity. During this shift, several opposing positions about hunting have emerged. In order to
understand the heated debate surrounding hunting in the
twenty-first century, it is important to understand the manner
in which the climate around the topic has changed.

Hunting, as discussed in this context, refers to the practice
of humans killing wild animals for provision of food, clothing, medicine, trophies, or recreation. Prior to the nineteenth-
and twentieth-century industrialization of the United States,
the majority of Americans lived in rural areas. A 1790 census
of U.S. citizens found that 95 percent of the population lived
in the countryside. By 1890, census data revealed that 35 percent of Americans lived in urban areas, and that number had
increased to 75 percent by 1990. The shift from rural to urban
living meant a change in lifestyle. In the 1790s, most Americans hunted animals for meat and grew crops to obtain veg-
etables, grains, and fruit. By 1990, the majority of Americans
no longer spent hours each day cultivating crops and obtain-

ing food through hunting. The industrial revolution, along with the advent of interstate railway transit, made a variety of food readily available to consumers.

As Americans moved to urban areas and spent less time in rural environments raising or hunting animals for food, the issues of animal cruelty and animal rights also became more prominent. In the 1950s, organizations such as the Humane Society of the United States were formed to prevent animal cruelty. By the early 1970s, the movement went a step further when a group of Oxford scholars began to question whether the moral status of nonhuman animals was necessarily inferior to that of human beings and whether animals should be entitled to their own basic rights and protections by law. In 1980, People for the Ethical Treatment of Animals (PETA) was formed; its slogan was, "Animals are not ours to eat, wear, experiment on, or use for entertainment."

The change in the role of hunting and the rise of the animal rights movement were mirrored by a shift in the portrayal of hunters in literature, movies, and the media. Early memoirs, books, and stories about hunting celebrated the hunter's skill and tracking ability against fierce animals and nature. Stories by author Ernest Hemingway and U.S. president Theodore Roosevelt in the 1920s recall the drama and action of hunting in Africa and the western United States as the heroes of the stories use their wits, strength, and cunning against wild animals. Recognizing the need to preserve natural habitat for animals, hunters also took an active role in the nature conservation movement in literature and the legislature. Roosevelt established the national parks system in the United States, and in 1929 the Game Law was passed to regulate the hunting of protected wild fowl and animals and to limit the seasons during which game or fowl could be hunted. On the whole, hunters in the early twentieth century were viewed in a romantic light as strong, moral, and skilled outdoorsmen.

In the 1940s and 1950s, the view of the hunter was mixed. In 1942, Walt Disney Studios released the animated movie *Bambi*, about a fawn. In a pivotal scene in the film, Bambi's mother is killed by a hunter, leaving young Bambi to fend for himself in the wild. Around the same time—in 1954 and 1955—Disney developed a television series based on the life of Davy Crockett called *Davy Crockett: King of the Wild Frontier*. The series celebrated Crockett's ability as a hunter and resulted in a children's fad of wearing coonskin caps and carrying toy Crockett buffalo rifles. The theme song cites Crockett's heroic deeds and upbringing with the lyrics: "Raised in the woods so he knew every tree, Kilt him a b'ar when he was only three. Davy, Davy Crockett, king of the wild frontier!" At the same time Elmer Fudd, the animated character from Warner Brothers, was created. Rather than being characterized as a strong, skilled hunter, however, Elmer is an inept hunter, creeping through the woods with a double-barreled shotgun to hunt rabbits, namely Bugs Bunny, but who instead ends up hurting himself.

By the 1980s and 1990s, hunters were portrayed in many films, books, and news reports as predominantly rural, lower class, and uneducated. Hunters found themselves stereotyped as "a bunch of big, burly guys who wear plaid and N.R.A. [National Rifle Association] caps and say, 'Let's go out and kill some defenseless animals,'" as one woman states in a 2004 *New York Times* article.

Hunting is now primarily a recreational activity or sport to be performed on weekends or vacations. In his book, *Mortal Stakes*, Jan Dizard concludes that the majority of hunters now hunt to "enjoy recreational benefits" while "sustain[ing] and embellish[ing] [their] appreciation for the ways wildlife and humans are indissolubly linked." However, the overall number of hunters is declining, according to a 2006 survey by the U.S. Fish and Wildlife Service. A large part of the decline is due to the trend of fewer children and teens learning to hunt.

Knowing the history of hunting in the United States is important for understanding the diverse points of view surrounding this often controversial subject. The four chapters in *Opposing Viewpoints: Hunting* provide contemporary perspectives on the following debates: Does Hunting Have a Place in the Twenty-First Century? How Have Modern Technological Advances Affected Hunting? Is Hunting an Important Part of Wildlife Maintenance? and Is Hunting a Form of Cruelty to Animals? In the following selections, contemporary viewpoints have been gathered in order to provide an evenhanded introduction to the issues surrounding hunting.

Does Hunting Have a Place in the Twenty-First Century?

Chapter Preface

In a Stone Age rock painting, a stampeding herd of deer is driven by beaters toward a line of bowmen. This painting depicts an integral part of prehistoric life: hunting. Prior to the spread of farming as a main method of food production around 8500 B.C., early humans obtained their food through hunting and gathering. Daily lives in these communities revolved around the capture and preparation of wildlife for food and raw materials used to make tools, weapons, clothing, and shelter. In addition, humans in this time period relied on hunting to protect themselves from wild animals. Survival of the community depended on the efficiency and success of the hunters. Accordingly, all male members of the tribe were taught to hunt.

Although the reliance on hunting for food decreased as more communities settled in villages and towns, the hunter's role still was important. Hunters obtained fresh meat to serve as a protein source and protected the settlements from dangerous wild animals. During times of crop failure or other agrarian shortfall, hunters used their skills to supplement the crops and livestock raised in villages. Hunting fulfilled community needs, and most male members of the community continued to be taught to hunt as a means of gathering food and providing protection.

In rural communities from 8500 B.C. to nineteenth-century America, hunting was still an integral part of daily life. In the twenty-first century, however, the vast majority of Americans live in cities or the suburbs rather than rural communities. Most of the food for the individuals settled in these metropolitan areas is produced on large-scale farms. Even the people still living in rural communities may not grow their own food. In fact, the majority of Americans—whether urban or rural—never see the living farm-raised plants and animals they purchase in the form of packaged meats and prewashed produce at the supermarket. There is, therefore, a significant separation between food producers and consumers in the United States. Hunting is no longer a necessary method of food acquisition for most modern families.

As society's need to obtain food by means of hunting has decreased, so has the need for protection from wild animals. In fact, hunting within city limits is often prohibited by law.

The shift in hunting from a necessity to a recreational activity in modern society has led to a vigorous debate over the place of hunting in a modern world. In the debate, several groups hold different positions on hunting. One group supports recreational hunting as a traditional outdoor activity that requires skill, patience, and knowledge. A second group feels that hunting is an integral part of wildlife conservation and management. Another position is held by a group that only supports hunting for human survival. A fourth group opposes hunting in all forms. In chapter 1, the authors debate the social, legal, and ethical roles of hunting and the hunter in the twenty-first century.

> "Hunting in and of itself requires no justification. The hunt is not only natural and healthful; it's an inextricable part of our heritage as human beings."

Hunting Is a Natural, Ethical, and Healthy Undertaking

Ward M. Clark

Ward M. Clark is a hunter, lecturer, and author of several nonfiction and fiction books. In this viewpoint, Clark discusses the reasons that modern humans hunt. Clark links historical and modern justifications for hunting to the larger view of hunting, which connects predator to prey and man to nature.

As you read, consider the following questions:

1. What human feature equips us best for hunting, in the author's view?
2. According to Clark, what contradictory aspect of hunting explains the relationship between human predator and animal prey?
3. Which characteristic of modern urban life does Clark assert results in a disconnect between humans and nature?

Modern hunters seem to find they are answering [the question "why hunt?"] frequently. Sometimes the question is put by the genuinely curious; sometimes it is a hostile demand for justification. In the first case, the answer is complex and thought provoking. In the second, the answer is simple—"because it suits me to do so." Hunting in and of itself requires no justification. The hunt is not only natural and healthful; it's an inextricable part of our heritage as human beings.

Man as Predator

Man is and has long been a terminal predator, as marvellously equipped for hunting by our intellect as a lion is by his claws and fangs, as a wolf by his swift legs and pack instinct. No matter whether humans today hunt directly, or employ middlemen to prepare their prey for them on farms and meat packing plants, the fact of our status as predator is in our very DNA. We owe the very fact of our world-conquering intellect on the hunt, on the stimulus that drove us to overcome the handicap of our clawless, blunt-toothed bodies, to develop weapons to match the feats of the greatest of animal predators; we owe our great brains to the access to high-quality diets of meat, marrow, and fat that predatory behaviour allowed.

But, the question remains nonetheless. Why, now, do we hunt?

Why Modern Man Hunts

Some hunt for the meat. A good reason in itself; game meat is lean, healthy, and free from additives; the process of obtaining it provides exercise and time in the outdoors, away from work pressures and the temptations of couches and televisions. The fruits of the hunt, properly cared for, are welcomed on the most discriminating of tables.

Some hunt for the camaraderie, another fine reason; for many of these, the actual hunt is secondary to the outing with friends, sharing the campfire with others of like mind and feeling. Another good reason; it is in the enjoyment of fine companions that we grow as social animals. The annual ritual of the mountain elk camp is a vital part of the year for many.

But, there is frequently another reason. A reason that's more compelling, and at the same time harder to explain.

A Tie to Nature

Henry David Thoreau, in the great classic *Walden*, wrote "Go fish and hunt far and wide day by day—farther and wider—and rest thee by many brooks and hearth-sides without misgiving. Remember thy Creator in the days of thy youth. Rise free from care before the dawn, and seek adventures. Let the noon find thee by other lakes, and the night overtake thee everywhere at home. There are no larger fields than these, no worthier games man may here be played." Thoreau spoke for many hunters in those words, hunters who hunt not solely for the meat, or for the company, but for the ageless, timeless experience of the hunt itself.

For it's true that for some of us the hunt is an answer in itself. It's enough to awake hours before the dawn, and to know the utter silence of a late autumn morning. To hear the crunch of snow under your boots as you begin the hike into the distant, silent mountains. To smell the pines along the trail, and see the silent sentinel spruces on the ridges, barely glimpsed in the pre-dawn dark. It's enough to sit, shivering, at that best spot on the top rim of a remote basin, watching the east grow bright, waiting for the first rays of warm sunshine to break though the trees and drive away the bitter cold of night.

But those moments, treasured as they are, pale before the ultimate goal of the hunt. It's a part of the hunter's soul, to carry the knowledge that somewhere, out among the pines, in the dark timber or the frost-covered meadows, a bull awaits, and the chance of the day may bring him within your awareness. The snap of a branch, the ghosting shape of antlers through the aspens, the sudden ringing bugle of a bull elk, as he appears, suddenly, where no bull was a moment before. His breath plumes out in the cold as he screams his challenge, and your hands and will freeze momentarily in awe of his magnificence.

It's enough to know that the day may bring the chance of a stalk, through the darkness under the trees, along the edges of the golden grasses of a meadow, creeping, creeping, under the streamside willows, silently, slowly, ever closer, testing the wind, watching underfoot for twigs, whispering a silent prayer to the forests and fields to allow you to close the gap, to make the shot.

With luck, you'll raise your rifle or draw your bow, and make your shot. More often than not, though, the bull escapes, to play the game of predator and prey another day, in another valley.

You can't buy moments like that; you can't find them on the Internet, or at the movie theatre. When the alarm rings in the icy cold of a pre-dawn tent at 9,000 feet, this type of hunter doesn't groan at the prospect of climbing out of the warm sleeping bag; instead, the prospects of the day are enough incentive to brave the cold, to pull on wool and leather, to step into the pitch-black outdoors, under ice-chip stars. It is with pleasure and anticipation that this hunter begins a day that will likely end back at the same tent, in the freezing dark, hours after sunset, at the end of a long hike out of the wild.

For hunting requires a level of participation unknown in any other human venture—hunting requires a communion with the very primal forces of Nature, taking life so that life may be. Hunting requires a contact that the non-hunter can never know, a contact with life itself. The hunter eschews supporting his or her life through a middleman; knowing the cost

Embracing Nature

Hunters choose to seek out and participate directly and personally in natural processes that are a daily part of the dynamic environment but that are obscure to most people in our society. As a recreation, hunting still provides food and other useful products, but the motivations to hunt extend far beyond subsistence. Its foremost amenities are a variety of personal satisfactions, including embracing the natural role of humans in a natural environment.

"Placing Hunting in Perspective,"
Wildlife Management Institute, 1996.
www.wildlifemanagementinstitute.org.

of one's diet, engenders respect for the lives that must be taken to sustain one's own life.

A Link to the Past

Early hunters knew this very well, as they revered their primary prey. For example, Plains Indians referred to the bison as "uncle" and "brother." Paleolithic cave drawings of game animals and hunt scenes are rendered with a loving reverence that is still evident today, thousands of years later. Modern hunters are much the same. Enter a hunter's home, and you'll likely find framed prints of deer and elk, waterfowl sculptures, photography of upland birds.

To some it seems contradictory; to express respect, reverence, even love for an animal that you pursue, hunt, kill, and eat. It's true that this seeming contradiction is as hard for hunters to explain as it is for non-hunters to understand.

An Understanding

Perhaps the answer lies in the very understanding of our role in Nature. Nature has but one law; Life feeds on Life, and Life gives Life to Life. People who obtain their steaks, chicken, and burgers from supermarkets and butcher's shops can lose sight of this fundamental truth, and perhaps they would prefer to have that process sanitized in just such a manner. In our modern, urbanized society, many like to imagine their own existence is bloodless, clean, and sanitary. But such an outlook is self-deluding.

The hunter knows very well the cost for the steaks that grace his plate. A year has been spent in preparation for the hunt, planning, caring for equipment, and practicing marksmanship. Without complaint or reservation, the hunter has arisen before dawn, as described above, and walked the many miles to where the game awaits. In the bright sun of a meadow, in the twilight of dusk, or in the shadows of the forest he has made the stalk, taken the shot with painstaking care, and dressed the animal. He has packed out quarters of elk, perhaps a two- or three-day process, often through rough, grueling country. The hunter has cared for hides and antler and meat, and the price for the meal of elk steak is ever with the one for whose life the elk's life has given way.

Most of all, the hunter has seen the sudden transition from a living animal to an inanimate food source, from animate life to meat for the table. The non-hunting urbanite likely has never seen this take place, and would not care to do so; but the hunter knows, with bittersweet regularity, the price that must be paid for continued existence.

It is for this very reason that the hunter reveres his prey. The intimate, timeless knowledge that Life springs from Life can only lead to reverence for the source of that Life. The bull elk in the dark timber, ghosting through the trees silently as smoke, will live on in the blood, bone and sinew of the hunter waiting on the ridge above; and the hunter, in his turn, will return to the Earth, to nourish the soil, to give rise to the grasses that will feed the elk. And how can the hunter not revere the greathearted bull, revere the magnificence of the great deer that will go to feed the hunter's family in the winter to come? Reverence for the game, reverence for the wellspring of life, reverence for the great, largely unknowable cycles of the Earth, all come from the intimacy with Nature found in the hunt.

Hunting Makes Us Human

Hunting is indeed what makes us human; hunting is what led humans to cooperate, to plan, to anticipate, to form society. The first great turning point in Mankind's development was when two unrelated families found they could hunt large animals by working together, and so be more efficient at obtaining high-quality food; thus was the first tribe born. Hunting has made us what we are.

It's unfortunate that the non-hunter often cannot see past the fact that the hunt results in the death of an animal. The death of an animal, it's true, is the goal of the hunt; but a greater goal is to be found in the overall experience, of which the actual kill is only the climactic moment. The hunter's soul often thrills as much, if not more, to the blown stalk, the bull that senses something amiss and vanishes into the mountains like a puff of smoke on the breeze, leaving no trace in his wake. Fond memories include the grouse that explodes from underfoot at the worst possible moment, the squirrel that set up a warning chatter in the penultimate seconds of a carefully planned approach. The vista of a great gulch viewed from the rim, with a herd of elk grazing peacefully, undisturbed, and totally unapproachable on the far side. And, indeed, in the final moment of success, when the hunter approaches, cautiously, the downed bull, lying still now against the bed of needles; the heart-pounding thrill of success, weighted against the bittersweet regret of the necessity of taking the life, facing the final truth that for life to be, another life must give way.

Life feeds on Life, and Life gives Life to Life. The hunter in success understands this great truth as no other human possibly can.

Why Hunt?

We hunt to pay homage to Nature, to Life, to the Earth. To make our annual pilgrimage to our beginnings, to lay hands on our heritage as members of the biotic community. To affirm once more that Life feeds on Life, and Life gives Life to Life. We hunt for the gift of an elk to a family, the gift of life from the Earth. In the hunt lies an affirmation, a recognition that we too will one day return to the Earth that has fed and nurtured us, and the elk will then feed on the minerals and nutrients returned to the soil from our bodies. That affirmation alone is enough for many of us who hunt, to send us once more out of our tents, trailers, and ranch houses, out into the freezing darkness under the glittering stars, to climb an unseen mountain for the chance at an elk.

Hunting has a fundamental truth that few non-hunters understand.

It's not about death. It's about life.

That's why.

> "Most hunting does not serve or promote vital human interests; therefore, most hunting is immoral."

Hunting Is Morally Permissible Only When It Is Necessary for Human Survival

Mark Rowlands

In this viewpoint, Mark Rowlands discusses his position that hunting is legitimate only when it is necessary for the preservation of the life or health of human hunters. He asserts that in all other cases hunting is morally wrong because it is counter to the vital interests of the animals being hunted and does not promote any essential human interest. Mark Rowlands is an author and lecturer in philosophy at Birkbeck College, University of London.

As you read, consider the following questions:

1. According to Rowlands, when is it morally acceptable for humans to hunt?

2. How does Rowlands respond to the argument that humans are morally correct to hunt animals in the same manner that animal predators prey on other animals?

Mark Rowlands, *Animals Like Us*. London: Verso, 2002, pp. 160–68. Copyright © Mark Rowlands. All rights reserved. Reproduced by permission.

3. When does human intervention become necessary
   to prevent one species in an environment from getting out of control, in Rowlands' view?

In the impartial position, it would be irrational to choose
any situation where a non-vital human interest is served or
promoted through the violation of a vital interest of an animal. This is because, in the impartial position, you do not
know whether you will be the human or the animal. Therefore, it is immoral, in the real world, to endorse such a situation. This is what makes animal husbandry, zoos, and vivisec-
tion, wrong. The same is true of hunting, at least in almost all
circumstances. Hunting, of course, involves killing animals,
and killing necessarily entails a thwarting of every vital (and,
for that matter, non-vital) interest the animal has. So, unless
the hunting serves or promotes human interests that are similarly vital, a world that contained hunting would be an irrational choice in the impartial position. Most hunting does not
serve or promote vital human interests, therefore most hunting is immoral.

When Is Hunting Legitimate?

Hunting is legitimate only when it serves or promotes vital
human interests. And this means, roughly, that hunting is permissible only when it is necessary for the preservation of the
life or health of the human hunters. For the vast majority of
humans, this is not the case. However, there are certain human societies, operating on the *margins of existence*, where
eating meat is essential to their survival. This is for the simple
reason that supplies of vegetable protein are scarce or non-
existent. The *Innuit* [native inhabitants of the Arctic and sub-
Arctic regions] provide an obvious example. In such cases, the
humans involved must be classified as, for all practical purposes, carnivores, creatures unable to survive without eating
meat. The impartial position allows that it is morally acceptable for such people to eat meat. In the impartial position, to

adopt a rule that proscribed eating meat for people such as the *Innuit* would be irrational; it would be to adopt a rule that potentially sealed one's own fate. More generally, the class of human beings who, for whatever reason, are unable to survive without eating meat should be treated along the same lines as any other carnivore. As we shall see in a moment, it is perfectly acceptable for such individuals to eat meat, nor do we have any obligation to assist the animals upon which they prey.

Limits on Subsistence Hunters

The scope of this rule, however, is strictly limited. It allows that humans who absolutely have to kill in order to live and be healthy may do so. But they may kill only what they need to satisfy their vital interests. If you are entitled to kill, say, fifty seals a year because you need these to survive, that's one thing. But it does not then follow that you have the right to kill a thousand seals so you can sell their pelts, or because someone else is paying you to do this because they want to take more fish. This falls outside the bounds of what is necessary for survival and health, and thereby falls outside the bounds of acceptable use.

In an ideal world, where everyone had the luxury of choosing where they lived, we might question someone who chooses to live in a place where killing animals was essential to survival. But it is, of course, not an ideal world. And, most people do not have this luxury. Certainly those living on the margins of existence don't. We have, it seems, far more pressing things to worry about—the animal husbandry techniques of big agribusiness, for example—than small numbers of humans, living on the margins of existence, who have to kill a small number of animals in order to survive.

Hunting for Pleasure

In specifying when hunting is permissible, I mentioned life and health. But what about something else that is, arguably, a

31

vital human interest? What about *happiness*? Some people claim that hunting is absolutely essential to their happiness, that a life without hunting is no life at all. Therefore, for those people at least, isn't hunting a vital interest? There are two points that count against this suggestion. First of all, it is not clear that happiness, in any full-blooded sense, is a vital interest on a par with life and health. Most people profess to be not particularly happy at all; there are very few people, however, who think that their lives are not worth living. Second, human interests are, if not infinitely, then at least indefinitely plastic. Whenever someone claims that one interest they have is of overriding importance and that, without it, life wouldn't be worth living then, basically, *they need to get out more!* Human happiness can be accommodated in various ways, and thinking that one particular way is of overriding importance almost always stems from the fact that one's experience is too narrow to provide an adequate basis for comparison.

Animals Kill to Eat, So Why Shouldn't Humans?

One of the most common defences of hunting is based around the idea that, in hunting animals, we are simply doing the same sort of thing that they do to each other. If the wolf's preying on the caribou is not morally wrong, then why should our preying on caribou be wrong? On the other hand, if our preying on caribou is morally wrong, then why would the caribou not have a case against the wolf?

One difference between us and wolves, of course, is that we are, while they are not, moral agents. They are unable to morally assess their actions by dispassionately evaluating them by way of the moral principles they adopt. Hence the wolf cannot be morally blamed for killing caribou for the simple reason that it is not the sort of thing that can be blamed. . . .

With regard to hunting, then, the crucial difference between humans and animals is that, in the vast majority of

Subsistence Hunting

Subsistence hunters hunt animals for food, skins and bone, and at some time in the history of all nations it was an essential way of obtaining food. Today, subsistence hunting is very important all over Africa. In Botswana bush meat (e.g. spring hares, small antelopes, birds) is an important source of protein for many people. Other regions where subsistence hunting is still important include the Arctic, and the rain forests of the Amazon and Central Africa.

Jocelyn Collins, "Hunting," EnviroFacts, 2001.
www.botany.uwc.ac.za/Envfacts/facts/hunting.htm.

cases, we don't have to hunt in order to survive, [but] they do. Except in the case of certain human beings, like the *Innuit*, occupying the margins of existence, vital human interests are not at stake. But when animals hunt, their vital interests are very much at stake. Therefore, human hunting practices cannot be justified by appeal to animal hunting practices.

Hunting Is Necessary to Eradicate "Pests"

One of the most common defences of hunting is based on the idea that it is necessary in order to keep down the numbers of "pests." What makes something a pest? [It is that its] characteristic behaviour impacts adversely on human interests, typically economic ones. This is probably the most common argument in favour of fox hunting in Britain. Foxes are pests, since their activities adversely affect the interests of farmers. Therefore, their numbers must be kept down. And, so the argument goes, hunting with dogs is the most effective way of doing this. Is this a good argument?

There are several things wrong with it. First, even if we accept that the numbers of foxes should be kept down (which, for reasons that will become clear in a moment, we should not), the question is not what is the most *effective* way of doing this, but what is the most *humane*. It is difficult to take seriously the claim that chasing an exhausted and terrified animal for miles across the countryside, before digging it out of its hole and either shooting it and/or allowing the hounds to tear it apart constitutes the most humane method at our disposal.

Second, just what is the farmer doing that his interests are adversely impacted by the activities of the fox? It's not as if the fox is nibbling away at his corn or wheat or barley. Rather, he is raising animals for food. Specifically, he is raising sheep. The vast majority of sheep are not raised for their wool; that would be financially unviable. They are raised for food. When they have reached market weight, they will be killed. Before this, many of them will be transported, indeed exported, often great distances in hot, cramped conditions, sometimes without food or water. If the arguments developed [here] . . . in general . . . are correct, then raising and killing animals for food is not a morally legitimate enterprise. And you cannot defend a practice like fox hunting on the grounds that it is necessary to preserve the profits you get from a morally illegitimate enterprise. That would be like a Mafia boss defending his killing of rivals on the grounds that it was necessary to protect his profits. If gains are ill-gotten, or earnings immoral, they cannot be used to justify a practice that is necessary in order to get or keep them.

Some animals, of course, do eat arable crops. Rabbits and rats, for example, will eat barley. Is it legitimate to hunt these in order to protect one's barley crop? Well, the first thing to do is compare the interests at stake. In most healthy arable systems—to the extent that one can use the term "healthy" in connection with the systems produced by modern arable production methods—the damage inflicted by rats, rabbits and other pests is fairly minimal. So, here we are looking at the vital interests of the rats and rabbits versus the economic interests of the farmer. So, this is a case of vital versus non-vital interests and, therefore, no contest. In certain circumstances, however, the number of rats, rabbits or other pests can get out of hand, and the economic damage they inflict can reach vital proportions. But then we have to ask why this happened. And the answer is, almost inevitably, because their natural predators—like, for example, foxes—have been hunted out of the locale. . . .

We have to stop trying to squeeze every ounce of yield we can out of our land. Then, reintroduce predators, wherever possible: foxes, polecats, wildcats, even the wolf and the bear. Not only will they make the British countryside a much more interesting place to be, they will also remove the need for any human culling of "pests."

Hunting Is Necessary for Conservation

Of all the arguments used to justify hunting, perhaps the most risibly perverse is the claim that it is necessary for conservation. Here's how the argument goes. If a certain number of animals are not hunted, there will be too many animals belonging to a given species for a given environment to support. The environment will then suffer through overgrazing, and the animals will die of starvation and disease.

What makes this argument so laughable, I think, is its wilful ignorance of certain basic facts, ones familiar to even young schoolchildren. Take, for example, the idea of the *balance of nature*. Very roughly, a given environment will settle down into a reasonably steady state, where the numbers of any given species are determined, therefore, kept in check by the numbers of members [of] other species that are related to it in sometimes complex relations of predation, competition, cooperation, and symbiosis. An environment that contains a certain amount of plant mass, for example, will support a certain number of, say, deer. But how many there [are] of these depends on how many members of directly competing species there are in the same environment and, of course, vice versa. It depends also on the numbers of predators there are and, again, vice versa. The relations of dependence are sometimes quite staggeringly complex, even awe-inspiring. But the basic idea is simple and well understood.

The idea that human intervention is generally necessary to prevent one species in an environment getting out of control is just ecologically ignorant. Sometimes this happens but when it does it is always because humans have first done something else: removed a major predator from the ecosystem. If you remove wolves from a given environment—as, for example, when humans systematically slaughtered virtually all the wolves in the contiguous forty-eight US states—then of course deer numbers will explode exponentially. *That was the whole point of the exercise!* Or at least one of them. That is, almost the only situations in which human culling of a given species is necessary in order to safeguard the environment, are situations that have been explicitly engineered by humans so that they can go and shoot lots of animals! The eradication of wolves from the contiguous forty-eight states in the early part of the twentieth century was partly to protect livestock but largely to increase the numbers of deer so that "sportsmen" would have more to shoot.

This is the whole philosophy—and I use the term loosely—behind game management. Take an environment. Remove the major predator or predators. Then you will have more "sport" animals to shoot. Shooting is then necessary, for, with their natural predators gone, their numbers would explode with devastating environmental consequences. However, you don't want to shoot all the sport animals. This would leave you with nothing to shoot next year. So, how many do you shoot? Kill only as many animals as will allow you to kill the same number next year. Then, in the long run, you will be able to kill *more* animals.

The idea that hunting animals can be justified on environmental grounds is a joke. Only if we remove large predators would this form of culling ever become necessary. And why would we remove large predators? Two reasons. Either we are protecting the profits from another morally illegitimate practice like animal husbandry. Or, we are deliberately creating the conditions under which we will have large numbers of animals to shoot. Not content with shooting deer, we want to stop everything else killing deer. Why? So we can shoot *more* deer. So we shoot the wolves to stop them competing with us, and thereby create the conditions where we can claim that killing deer is necessary on environmental grounds. This claim should be treated with the contempt it deserves.

Hunting thwarts the most vital interests of the animals hunted. However, in the vast majority of cases, it does not serve or promote any similarly vital human interest. In the impartial position, choosing a situation where vital interests are outweighed or overridden by non-vital interests would be irrational. Therefore, hunting, in the vast majority of cases, is morally wrong. The traditional arguments used to support hunting do not work, and some of them are positively risible.

> "Hunting teaches us that, like all life-forms, we are dependent upon the integrity and viability of nature."

Modern Hunters Are Stewards of Wildlife and the Environment

Randall L. Eaton

In this viewpoint, Randall Eaton discusses the role of hunters as protectors of wildlife and the environment. Eaton emphasizes the innate human instinct to hunt and the way in which hunting connects humans to animals and the environment. Randall Eaton is an expert on animal behavior and wildlife conservation as well as an award-winning author, professor, lecturer, and film producer.

As you read, consider the following questions:

1. What programs do hunting licenses and federal excise taxes fund, according to Eaton?
2. What does Eaton say that hunters learn about themselves and the world when they kill their first animal?

Randall L. Eaton, "Why Hunting Is Good Medicine for Youth, Society, and the Environment," *Outdoor Edge Magazine*, 2006. Reproduced by permission of Randall L. Eaton, www.randalleaton.com.

3. In Eaton's view, what impact does hunting have on a man's tendency toward aggression and violence?

Depending on whose figures you use, [in 2006] there are at least 38 to 45 million hunters and fishers in the U.S. They are among the most prominent and influential of all demographic groups. Their total economic contribution is $70 billion annually, $179 billion in ripple effect. They support more jobs than the largest Fortune 500 company, and rank as the 11th largest corporation in America. Each year they generate six times more gold and silver than Hollywood's top 40 movies of all time.

Hunters' Contributions

Five million more Americans fish than golf. In a time when commercial fishing is fingered for depleting fish stocks worldwide, the real fish story is that sportfishing generates nearly ten times more revenue than commercial fishing. They spend more but use much less of the resource.

License sales and federal excise taxes on rods and reels and firearms and ammunition pay for most of the bill for fisheries and wildlife conservation and management.

Hunters and fishers contribute up to $1.7 billion each year for conservation. For over 60 years, they have paid this self-imposed tax totaling more than $7.6 billion for protection of our natural environment and fish and wildlife. Since 1934, when the first duck stamp was purchased, more than $647 million has gone to conserving over 5 million acres of wildlife habitat, greater in size than the State of Massachusetts, providing breeding and wintering grounds for waterfowl and countless other species, most of them non-game.

Hunters as Conservationists

Volunteer hunters make up groups like Ducks Unlimited, which by itself has purchased over 10 million acres of wetlands habitat in North America. In less than 20 years, Rocky

Mountain Elk Foundation has acquired millions of acres for elk and other wildlife, game and non-game. It has launched successful programs to reestablish elk throughout the midwest and eastern U.S. The National Wild Turkey Federation has established wild turkey populations across the continent. There are more deer and turkeys [in 2006] than at any time in history.

Consider this: for every one of its 700,000 members, Ducks Unlimited has purchased about 15 acres of productive wildlife habitat to the benefit of the entire community of living things. If these men and women can translate their love of nature, which was fostered in a duck blind when they were young, into hundreds of millions of dollars to protect the living earth in a time when the sheer insanity of [the] expanding economy threatens the survival of the biosphere, what do you think five million of them might do? Or fifty million?

A Decline in Numbers

The remarkable list of achievements of North American hunters and anglers goes on, but, tragically, at the very time when the earth needs them most, the recruitment of youth into hunting is dwindling. Nine of ten hunters are now over forty, which means that in a few years recreational hunting may cease to exist. The decline in the ranks of hunters is due in part to a lack of understanding of the relationship between hunting and stewardship of the environment. What happens inside hunters that motivates them to work together and take responsibility for the environment? Much of the blame goes to hunters themselves, who have failed to articulate the inner side of hunting and communicate it effectively to nonhunters.

Hunting Is Justifiable

From the perspective of economy, ecology and environmental conservation, hunting is important and justifiable. However necessary, these justifications are not sufficient to win the day.

Hunters as Wildlife Stewards

Hunting has been good for wildlife, both directly and indirectly, not because individual hunters consciously harness themselves to broad wildlife management goals, but because hunters have been effective lobbyists for the critters they love to hunt. Many hunters also have an environmental sensibility that extends well beyond their narrow self-interest, but that is a separate matter. What counts is that the men and women who love to hunt grouse or deer or elk or whatever have been willing to pay for research and habitat enhancement and to accept restrictions on their own hunting in order to ensure that game animals prosper.

Jan E. Dizard, Mortal Stakes:
Hunters and Hunting in Contemporary America.
Amherst: University of Massachusetts Press, 2003.
Copyright © 2003 by University of Massachusetts Press.

The community of hunters has emphasized the effects of recreational hunting, not actually why they hunt or what hunting does for them as human beings. In so doing they have left out the very heart of hunting. The impressive economic impact of hunting and its unparalleled record in environmental conservation reflect the profound psycho-spiritual influence of hunting. If we want men who respect life and take responsibility for the environment, then we must be aware of what hunting does for the male heart.

The hunt is as archetypal to males as birthing is to females. The hunt marries young men to wild animals and nature just as birthing bonds a young woman to children and life. Men are adapted to take life to serve life. Hunting itself teaches universal virtues, and the taking of life opens hearts and engenders respect and responsibility.

Both males and females may benefit much from hunting and fishing (fishing is hunting with a hook), but boys especially gain from hunting. Initiation to adulthood is inborn and automatic for women: they leave childhood and become capable of reproduction with the onset of menses. Not so for boys who during adolescence are compelled to prove themselves worthy as men. For hundreds of thousands of years, boys have proved themselves worthy by killing a wild animal of sufficient size. That demonstrates to prospective brides, in-laws and society their ability to protect and provide.

Hunting Instinct

The instinct to hunt appears early in males. A German scientist examined behavior in over 60 cultures worldwide. He observed in them all that boys between the age of 4 and 5 spontaneously begin to throw rocks, often competing with one another in terms of accuracy or distance. Cultural conditioning cannot explain the boys' behavior, since in many of the cultures adult males do not throw rocks or anything else. Moreover, girls did not exhibit this behavioral pattern. Surely boys are programmed to begin developing weapon skills early in life, a reflection of the long history of hunting among human males. We can be equally certain that the original weapons of our earliest human ancestors were rocks.

Form follows function in evolution, and the human is no exception. The male shoulder is constructed differently than the female's and better suited for throwing, another indication of the male's adaptation to hunting. Whether [former] President Jimmy Carter or staunch anti-hunter Cleveland Amory, most civilized men killed a bird or other small animal as a child. Normally they did so before [being] initiated to hunting, and many had never seen anyone else hunt or kill an animal. They use rocks, slingshots, bows or air rifles.

Just as females are biologically adapted to reproduce, males are adapted to hunt, kill and provide. The instinct propels them to pursue the animal, but a surprise awaits them. The same happens to a young man whose rampant sex drive pushes him towards a sexual encounter. His surprise comes when he falls in love, not at all what he anticipated. And that is the way normal human development moves, from lower to higher, in this case, from sexual instinct (eros) to spiritual love (agape).

From sex to love and marriage, the path to fatherhood tempers a man's passion, opens his heart and teaches him compassion. The path of the hunt leads from instinct to the kill. The death of the animal evokes a strong mix of emotions and self-reflection. It is an ambiguous moment for most males who, according to surveys I've conducted, feel a combination of elation, sadness and pride.

A Connection to Nature

In the same way that young children spontaneously imitate the gestures, postures and sounds of animals, the young hunter identifies with the animals he hunts. He studies them, tracks them, listens for them, anticipates them, calls them, even dreams them. When the moment of truth arrives, the young man is caught off guard at the sight of the beautiful beast, bloodied, soiled and lifeless. In an eternal moment, he realizes that he, too, is mortal and impermanent. At the deepest level he is stunned by the awareness that despite all appearances to the contrary he and the animal are essentially one, part of something far greater than themselves. It is a supreme moment of humility that launches a boy's spiritual life and connects him to nature.

The young hunter is also keenly aware that the animal died for him, for his passage to manhood and for the sustenance of his body and spirit. It is a holy communion, the original sacrificial rite that opens a young man's heart and fills him with empathy. "Thinking with the heart" means that when we hunt we learn to listen to our deepest feelings and honor them. That is why over 90% of the mature hunters I've surveyed report letting suitable specimens go, often because it simply doesn't feel right to kill them.

As one who serves life by taking life, the young hunter adopts a serious commitment to temper his passion, the origin of ethical life. For him the wild animal is a blessed gift. The hunt teaches a spirit of gratitude to the animals and for the gifts of nature as well as to life itself and the divine. Most older hunters report that they thank the animals they've taken as well as the Creator.

Lessons Learned

Hunting invokes an altered state of consciousness, one of supreme alertness to the animal and the environment. It gets us out of ourselves, beyond our ego, and as a consequence the hunt is fundamentally a religious experience, one that reconnects us to the source. Hunting teaches the interconnection and interdependence of all life, not in an abstract, intellectual sense, but at the deepest level of knowing. Like men of hunting-gathering societies, recreational hunters know from direct experience that interdependence is a fact of life.

Because hunting reveals the impermanence of life and our own mortality, the taking of an animal's life evokes respect for all life, animal and human alike. Killing an animal teaches us the terrible extent of our power, and so it evokes responsibility.

For these reasons, leading authorities in family therapy, male development, adolescent psychology and teen violence agree that shooting sports and hunting are good for youth. Michael Gurian, best-selling author of several books on how to properly raise boys into fine young men, agrees with Dr. Jim Rose, neuropsychologist at the University of Wyoming, that not only is hunting unrelated to aggression and violence, it produces less violent, more peaceful men. . . .

Hunting teaches us that, like all lifeforms, we are dependent upon the integrity and viability of nature.

Though the hunt is goal-oriented, it teaches us that all of creation functions by processes and that we are part of the process. It engenders a "7th generation perspective," making decisions today with future generations in mind. As [Native American] Athabascan elder, Peter John, said, "The animals you take are important to your grandchildren." Because hunters are motivated to "fiercely protect nature," as poet Robert Bly said, they are the leaders in environmental conservation.

Hunting teaches us to be observant and patient, to emulate nature and slow down, to "be here now" in the present moment. It teaches us that inner peace and sanity are possible in an insane world. According to Don Jacobs, a leading thinker in education, "Hunting is the ideal way to teach young people universal virtues including patience, generosity, courage, fortitude and humility."

The hunt promotes genuine self-confidence, tempered by humility and gratitude, as well as self-sufficiency. It teaches us self-restraint in the use of lethal weapons.

The hunt naturally promotes ethics universally associated with aboriginal and recreational hunting. The First Precept of Buddhism is known as "ahimsa," which actually means "to avoid causing unnecessary harm," which to hunters means taking only what they need and using what they take. It also means minimizing the suffering of animals. The first vow of Zen Buddhism is to save all life, the equivalent among hunters of "putting back," stewardship of the environment.

The hunt submerges us in the subtle realities of life. These include the power of prayer, envisioning what we want, tempered by ethical choice. Every hunt is a prayer in motion, and seasoned hunters know that faith in the outcome has much to do with success. Hunting teaches us the significance of attitude, intention and right-mindedness.

These are some of the secrets hidden deep in hunting, the original rite of passage for which there is no substitute and the only path of initiation that marries men to the 'other' that is nature. Those who directly participate in the food chain enter into the Great Mystery of life as life *and* death. For them the sacred hunt is a love chain.

More than at any time in the history of the world we need men who are deeply wedded to nature, which is to say that we need men who value the viability of the entire biological community above consumerism and the unsustainable economy that feeds it. Hunters are such men. Their unparalleled performance on the front lines of conservation makes them the ideal model for a world in crisis.

> *"[Hunting is] bloodlust and dominance. It's arrogance and selfishness. It's hatred and brutality. It's dishonor and viciousness. It's murder and it's obscene."*

Hunting Is Murder

Gary Yourofsky

In this viewpoint, animal rights activist Gary Yourofsky outlines the weaknesses in arguments used by hunters to justify hunting. Yourofsky refutes the notion that hunting is necessary to control overpopulation. He states that any overpopulation problems were originally caused by policies created by hunters and executives pandering to hunters. Gary Yourofsky is an animal rights activist and lecturer, and the founder of the animal rights organization Animals Deserve Absolute Protection Today and Tomorrow (ADAPTT).

As you read, consider the following questions:

1. According to Yourofsky, what policies resulted in an overpopulation of deer in Michigan?

2. What impact has the Deer Range Improvement Program had on the size of deer herds, in Yourofsky's view?

3. How does Yourofsky respond to the claim that
hunting protects animals from starvation?

I am the founder and president of Michigan's most outspoken and uncompromising humanitarian organization,
ADAPTT [Animals Deserve Absolute Protection Today and
Tomorrow]. Nearly 80 high schools and universities have invited me to educate and enlighten students about animal liberation, ethics, justice and kindness.

Perspectives on Animals and Humans

Before I refute every hunting lie, let me begin with two quotes
from some well-known animal rights activists.

The first one is from [Indian political and spiritual leader]
Mohandas Gandhi. "The life of a lamb is no less precious than
that of a human being. The more helpless the creature is, the
more it is entitled to protection from the cruelty of humans."

The second quote [is] from the great philosopher Pythago-
ras: "As long as humanity continues to be the ruthless de-
stroyer of other beings, we will never know health or peace.
For as long as people massacre animals, they will kill each
other. Indeed those who sow the seed of murder and pain will
never reap joy and love."

Hunting Lies and Realities

Now, contrary to the rosy picture hunters always paint about
themselves—the noble hunter, the honest hunter, the caring
hunter, the concerned hunter—let's run down a quick list of
noble hunting adages: Shoot more and shoot more often, I'm
a gut-pile addict, whack 'em and stack 'em, live to hunt/hunt
to live and kill on.

And how about this comment from Ted Nugent, the
world's most outspoken animal-killer and just about every
hunter's hero: "I contribute to the dead of winter and the
moans of silence, blood trails are music to my ears. I'm a gut-

pile addict. The pig didn't know I was there. It's my kick. I love shafting animals. It's rock 'n' roll power."

It's hard for animal rights humanitarians to discuss the truth about hunting when we're constantly dealing with lies about overpopulation, lies about kindness and lies about science.

Hunters and Policy

ADAPTT is fed up with hunters, their government cronies and all of their sick mentalities. The so-called "experts" who work for the DNR [Michigan Department of Natural Resources] and the NRC [National Research Council] are not "experts." They're hunters and hunt supporters.

And hunting is not sound science. It is only sound fun for unsound individuals who commit cowardly acts. And it sounds to me that any sound person who possesses a scintilla of sound sense would understand that soundly truth.

To appease hunters in 1971, the DNR began serious efforts to change the "old forest" situation in Michigan. There were around 500,000 deer at that time, which wasn't enough to please the hunters. Therefore, the DNR instituted the Deer Range Improvement Program known as DRIP, which called for the clear-cutting of 1.2 million acres of forest, creating a more accessible food supply for deer [so as to] further stimulate reproduction. The DNR also has always issued a disproportionate number of licenses to kill male deer, because killing males instead of females causes the females' internal reproductive mechanism to go haywire. Then, she ends up giving birth to twins and even triplets to keep the species going.

The DRIP program and sex-biased hunting has caused the deer herd to level out at around 2 million animals last year.

For the record, hunters cause an increase in deer-car accidents and contribute to crop damage.

No Chance for Escape

Hunting by humans operates perversely. The kill ratio at a couple hundred feet with a semi-automatic weapon and scope is virtually 100 percent. The animal, no matter how well-adapted to escape natural predation (healthy, alert, smart, quick, etc.) has virtually no way to escape death once it is in the cross hairs of a scope mounted on a rifle. Nature's adaptive structures and behaviors that have evolved during millions of years simply count for naught when man is the hunter.

Peter Muller, "Hunting by Humans Perverse, Too Efficient—Nature Has Solutions," All Creatures. www.all-creatures.org/cash/sa-perverse.html.

In 1972, there were 10,742 deer-car collisions. In 2000, there were about 70,000. Gee, I thought hunters were hunting to reduce deer-car collisions? In 1996, The Michigan Farm Bureau even threatened to file a class-action lawsuit against the DNR for solely catering to the needs of hunters.

By the way, as deer-car accidents and crop damage steadily increased over the years, here's what Dave Arnold, a DNR executive, had to say to the *Detroit Free Press* on January 1, 1980: "Don't lose sight of the purpose of the program. When the DNR decided several years ago to try and increase the herd to about one million animals, we knew the auto collision rate and crop damage would rise."

Overpopulation Problem Grows

Here's what Ned Caveney, a DNR state forester, had to say to the *Northwoods Call*, a Charlevoix paper, on May 26, 1991: "In Michigan, we manipulate forest habitat to produce amazingly unnatural deer numbers—up to two million of the critters some years. That probably approaches two million more than existed before man got into the act."

In the '90s, pro-hunting governor John Engler created The Hunting and Heritage Task Force in order to expand hunting and fishing opportunities to the public, which is the same reason why the U.S. Fish and Wildlife Service exists. By the way, the USFWS offers 290 hunting programs and 307 fishing programs on the 514 national wildlife refuges throughout the U.S.

In paragraph six of Engler's Hunting and Heritage Task Force edict, it states the following: "While Michigan offers widespread opportunities to hunt and fish, more could be done to encourage participation, especially in high-population centers. All divisions within the DNR should work together, making hunting and fishing more accessible on both public and private lands. Where possible, expand opportunities to hunt and fish within urban parks and recreation areas."

This was the sole purpose behind the recent deer killings at our metro-parks. Not because the deer were eating up all the trillium plants. The HCMA [Huron-Clinton Metropolitan Authority] board of commissioners wouldn't know the difference between trillium and helium. Moreover, humans are the only animals who destroy land and take more than they need.

The metro-park killings didn't take place because the hunters wanted to donate food to the hungry. That's just a clever public relations gimmick to try and place a halo around those who murder animals for fun. It is far more cost-efficient to feed hungry people spaghetti and stir-fried tofu, and you can feed more people that way too.

Wildlife Management and Hunters

Everyone must understand that wildlife management is an illusory concept created around 100 years ago. There is no such thing as wildlife management. Humans cannot manage nature. The only managing humans should be doing is managing to stay out of the animals' space.

And, once again, it is unjust, stupid and contemptible that the DNR and NRC—made up entirely of hunters and hunt supporters—make decisions about the fate of wild animals. That would be akin to allowing pedophiles to write child protection laws and misogynists [to] pen domestic abuse laws.

Do hunters eat their kills? Yes. But do hunters hunt for food? No! They hunt for the thrill of the kill. They receive a rush. A super-shot of adrenaline. It's bloodlust and dominance. It's arrogance and selfishness. It's hatred and brutality. It's dishonor and viciousness. It's murder and it's. obscene.

Hunters always use the excuse that deer are going to starve to death during the winter as if starvation wasn't a natural process and nature's way of controlling populations and the ecosystem's way of working.

Starving deer provide food for scavenger animals and is nature's way of weeding out sickly animals and allowing the strongest ones to reproduce.

A bullet to the head or an arrow through the chest is not a solution to starvation. But, furthermore, hunters don't even shoot starving deer. They don't make good trophies and don't have lots of meat.

I dare anyone to show me a photograph of one hunter last year who shot one emaciated deer. Just one. Hunters shoot big bucks with big racks for big trophies. Watch their TV shows on PBS and ESPN and TNN. That's all they talk about—big racks and big trophies.

On April 17, 1989, in the *Free Press*, Nugent said this about hunting: "I don't hunt for meat. I hunt to hunt."

In 1990, Nugent said the following in his *World Bowhunters Magazine*: "Nobody hunts just to put meat on the table because it's too expensive, time-consuming and extremely inconsistent."

For the record, I never threatened to harm someone's child over the recent deer-killings in our metro-parks. I threatened to take a bullet for the deer and form my own deer-police unit to protect deer from hunters. But I did challenge about six sissified animal-killing hunters to show me how tough "tough guys" really are. I wanted to fight these bullies and put them in their place. Unfortunately, as usual, they refused to take me up on my challenge. If there's one thing that I've learned in six years of intense activism, animal-abusers are cowards who would never fight someone who would fight back.

> *"I increasingly find that where I become a stronger hunter, I become a more proficient Marine, particularly in my self-sufficiency, confidence and ability to interpret a challenge from a perspective outside my own."*

Childhood Hunting Skills Make Better Soldiers

Brian Donlon

In this viewpoint, Brian Donlon discusses the hunting skills and lessons he learned in childhood and their application to his current military career. He notes that the learned qualities of self-sufficiency, confidence, and perspective have allowed him to be a more effective marine. Donlon is an avid hunter and a captain in the United States Marine Corps.

As you read, consider the following questions:

1. How does self-sufficiency help a hunter or a Marine succeed, in Donlon's view?
2. According to Donlon, how is it best to learn the skills of planning, patience, and endurance in both hunting and in the military?

Brian Donlon, "Well of Confidence," *Outdoor Life*, vol. 21, no. 1, December 2006–January 2007, p. 114. Copyright © Dec. 2006–Jan. 2007 Time Inc. Reproduced by permission.

3. What role does the learned ability to look at situations from a different perspective serve in the military, in Donlon's opinion?

Growing up, I spent every summer at my grandparents' farm in Virginia. All of my memories of these trips include hours spent ranging along oak-lined ridges and across fields of tall grass and bramble, pellet rifle always in hand. In those sun-drenched, humid summer days, I entertained two fantasies. The first was of hunting big game as Theodore Roosevelt did, across continents and in exotic locales; the second was of earning the right to call myself a United States Marine. Every deer track and turkey feather I encountered seemed solid proof of my growing ability in the wild, each shot from my rifle a testament that I too could be part of the brotherhood that fought "in any clime or place."

These days, my time spent wandering freely through the hills has become more precious than ever, for while I have long since abandoned my hope of becoming a professional hunter, I have been honored to serve as a Marine over the last four years.

A Complementary Skill Set

Nonetheless, while one dream has fallen in the wake of the other, I still see a complementary nature between my life as a hunter and my life as a Marine. I increasingly find that where I become a stronger hunter, I become a more proficient Marine, particularly in my self-sufficiency, confidence and ability to interpret a challenge from a perspective outside my own.

I define self-sufficiency as a collection of individual disciplines that allows me to succeed amid the stresses of fatigue and discomfort. The qualities needed to spend a cold desert night watching a sliver of road from the muddy edge of a reed-filled canal are the same as those that keep a hunter silent and patient for hours in a tree stand, though everything

Enthusiastic Child Hunters

After the hunt, the young boy was asked if he felt bad about shooting his first deer. Paraphrasing his answer, he said: "Shooting a deer was one of the most exciting things I've ever done. I don't feel bad at all because our family loves to eat the meat."

Next, the reporter posed a different question to a bright teenage girl nearing her 16th birthday: "If you had the choice of either going deer hunting with your father or getting your driver's license and taking the car out with your friends, which would you choose to do?"

"Deer hunting with Dad!" she answered without hesitation. "I can go out with my friends any time, but hunting is special!"

Duncan Dobie, ". . . The Mouth of Babes,"
Petersen's Hunting, August 2006, pp. 34–35.

about the wind-frozen morning he endures tells him to seek cover and warmth far from the lonely deer trail he watches. Such qualities do not come free with the purchase of a hunting license, nor, despite the myth, are they permanent characteristics of boot camp. Planning, patience and endurance are learned through repetition. In my case, the repetition came on those afternoons spent scouting for signs and those mornings spent tramping through snow searching for a wounded deer. Later, this same germ of self-sufficiency would serve as the start of deeper disciplines I would use as a Marine.

Memories Provide Confidence

Hemingway once wrote of a soldier returning from World War I and the confidence he felt when he remembered "all of the times that had been able to make him feel cool and clear inside himself when he thought of them; the times so long back when he had done the one thing, the only thing for a man to do, easily and naturally, when he might have done something else."

The last day I hunted for whitetail deer was four winters ago. Many times in the three deployments that have separated me from that afternoon, I have closed my eyes and thought of the buck crossing over the ridgetop and pushing toward my stand, his feet rustling the graying leaves along the trail. I can still hear the sound of the single gunshot and feel the recoil of the weapon in the instant before the deer fell.

The buck was not exceptional in size of body or rack, nor was the shot taken at a great distance. Yet confidence still projects from this memory, for the moment was unmarred by ambiguity or doubt. A hunt was planned, an afternoon was spent in the pursuit and the goal was achieved. There was no question in the end, only the certainty of success. This incident is an example of the small moments of confidence born of my hunts that built upon one another and thus, in the times when I was most challenged by fear, fatigue, homesickness and stress, provided a well, a reservoir of confidence from which I drew.

Important Lessons in Perspective

I have been taught many times that "the enemy has a vote," that the best plan is one that understands the enemy. Whether you're seeking bear along mountain slides or protecting a convoy route, any plan that doesn't account for the opponent's point of view leaves the chance of success to luck alone. I first faced the challenge of a competitor with keen senses and a superior knowledge of the terrain in my early years of hunting, those years when it seemed impossible to fill a tag. For two seasons I hunted without getting a deer. It was not until I "turned the map around" and forced myself to understand the ground from a deer's perspective that I finally achieved success.

Once in Iraq, these lessons took on a new pattern. Bedding areas, wind and food sources were replaced by weapons caches, historic IED [improvised explosive device] sites and trigger lines, the signs left by a new competitor in a much more dangerous game.

Just as the role of the hunter and that of the warrior were one and the same in our primal past, when procuring and protecting a food source was central to survival, there is no clear delineation between the qualities that make me a good hunter and those that make me a good Marine. My makeup as a Marine has been undeniably molded by my days spent hunting, providing a source of comfort in trying times, valued experience in the face of adversity and a base on which to build greater strength.

"The Humane Society of the United States is opposed to all sport hunting because we believe that killing animals for fun has no place in a civilized and humane world. [This] recent effort compounds animal exploitation with the exploitation of children."

Hunting Is Recruiting Children to Slaughter Defenseless Wildlife

Heidi Prescott

In this viewpoint, Heidi Prescott discusses the dangers of lowering the minimum hunting age to eight years old. Prescott notes that if even seasoned hunters have hunting accidents, children will surely be at risk for accidents and injury. The viewpoint asserts that sport hunting is inhumane and allowing children to hunt constitutes exploitation. Heidi Prescott is senior vice president for campaigns of the Humane Society of the United States.

Heidi Prescott, "Cheney Accident Shows Why 8-Year-Olds Shouldn't Hunt," *Milwaukee Journal Sentinel*, February 19, 2006, www.jsonline.com. Reproduced by permission of the author.

As you read, consider the following questions:

1. What lesson does Prescott feel can be learned from Vice President Dick Cheney's 2006 hunting accident?

2. What safety requirement does Prescott suggest be implemented if the minimum hunting age is lowered?

3. According to Prescott, why might a child be at greater risk for hunting accidents?

L egislation is now pending in Wisconsin that would lower the minimum hunting age from 12 to 8.

There also is a timely lesson to be learned from the recent [February 2006] hunting accident in which Vice President Dick Cheney accidentally shot and wounded Harry Whittington, one of his hunting companions. But it is a lesson that a well-financed and politically sophisticated hunting lobby is working hard to keep the public from learning.

The lesson is this: Hunting is a very dangerous pursuit, no matter who is doing it. Cheney and Whittington are both frequent hunters with many years of experience in the field. If they can be involved in an accidental shooting, everyone who hunts is at risk.

Recruiting Children

The hunting lobby wants the public to believe that hunting is safe because they are in the midst of a national campaign called "Families Afield," designed to entice children into hunting, especially deer hunting, which is the most popular and the most profitable form of hunting in America.

Despite pious talk about heritage and tradition, the effort is an exercise in raw greed.

Hunting is a $21 billion-a-year business, and the number of hunters in America has been declining steadily for the past 30 years. Unless this trend can be reversed, the hunting indus-

Hunting Makes People Callous

"Hunting breeds insensitivity to the suffering of others, whether animal or human," says Susie Cutler, 39, a Porter, Ind., lawyer who demonstrates against hunters in a nearby state park. "You can look at some of the shooting rampages in schools—a lot of [these kids] were taught to hunt by adults. In their minds, killing is a viable option" in dealing with problems.

Lance Morrow, "Should Kids Hunt?"
Time, *November 30, 1998.*

try, including the manufacturers and sellers of firearms and ammunition, is going to see its profits go into a tailspin.

The centerpiece of their campaign to put deer rifles—which can easily kill a human being a mile away—in the hands of small children is a legislative proposal that is being introduced in state capitals around the country. This hunting industry legislation would do away with any minimum hunting age for children.

Minimal Safety Precautions

The only requirement would be that a parent be within arm's length of the child. Cynically, the industry argues that parents know best when a child is mature enough to use a firearm, and the government has no business interfering in what should be a family matter.

This is rank insanity. In every state, a person has to be 21 before he or she can drink. No one argues that parents should decide when their children are old enough to drink because everyone knows that while some families would make responsible decisions, some would not and the potential consequences for the community are too great.

Nationwide, children have to be at least 15 and, in many cases, 16 before they can drive a car. No one would suggest that a child of 10 or 11 be allowed to drive as long as a parent was in the front passenger seat, within arm's length.

Risks for Accidents

Hunters have to make snap decisions to shoot or not to shoot under conditions of extreme emotional pressure. When a deer breaks into a clearing or a bird flushes in a whir of wings, there is no time for a child to ask a parent what to do. There is no time for a parent to restrain a child who is unwittingly, in the heat of the moment, about to shoot a human being.

The Humane Society of the United States is opposed to all sport hunting because we believe that killing animals for fun has no place in a civilized and humane world. But this recent effort compounds animal exploitation with the exploitation of children.

If you're inclined to believe the hunting lobby when they claim that hunting is safe, even for children, look at the matter of Cheney and Whittington, two seasoned and savvy hunters.

The bill lowering the minimum hunting age in Wisconsin from 12 to 8 is pending [in February 2006] before the state Senate. It is our hope that due in part to this recent tragedy, it has the good sense to shoot this bill down.

Periodical Bibliography

The following articles have been selected to supplement the diverse views presented in this chapter.

Animal Liberation Front — "The Fallacy of Sport Hunting," undated. www.animalliberationfront.com/Practical/Fishing--Hunting/Hunting/FallacyofSportHunting.htm.

Tom Dickson — "Hunting Myths: Dispelling Some Myths About Hunting," Minnesota Department of Natural Resources, 2007. www.dnr.state.mn.us/hunting/tips/myths.html.

Duncan Dobie — ". . . The Mouths of Babes: Children Allow the Real Tradition of Hunting to Shine on National Television," *Hunting*, August 2006.

Bob Hendricks — "How to Reason with an Anti-Hunter," HuntingNet.com, undated. www.hunting.net/articles.

Lisa Kemmerer — "Hunting Tradition: Treaties, Law, and Subsistence Killing," undated. http://animalliberationfront.com/Saints/Authors/Essays/essays.htm.

Colman McCarthy — "Ten Cliches to Make a Hunter Happy," *National Catholic Reporter*, December 16, 2005.

National Shooting Sports Foundation Inc. — "The Ethical Hunter," 2006. http://familiesafield.org/pdf/The_Ethical_Hunter.pdf.

Bob Reeves — "Religions Differ on Attitudes Toward Hunting," *Lincoln Journal Star*, November 12, 2006.

Wayne van Zwoll — "Why Hunting Can't Be What It Was," North American Hunting Club, 2007. www.hunting-club.com.

Gary Yourofsky — "Hunters Are the Terrorists of the Animal World," undated. www.animalliberationfront.com.

OPPOSING
VIEWPOINTS®
SERIES

CHAPTER 2

How Have Modern Technological Advances Affected Hunting?

Chapter Preface

In December 1994 a successful Texas banker quit his job in order to create and market a battery-powered duck with flapping wings and paddling feet called the "Wonderduck." The Wonderduck was not created as a toy; it is a hunting lure designed to encourage real ducks to land within shooting range of a hunter. Following the principles of this invention, several other robotic ducks with variations of spinning, flapping, and splashing wings have been created to mimic the Wonderduck. The robotic ducks are indeed more effective than the older wooden lures, and one U.S. field study found that the robotic decoy ducks attracted ten more ducks per hour than a stationary decoy duck. The effectiveness of the robotic ducks stimulated a vigorous debate among duck hunters and, eventually, lawmakers. Several states, including Washington and Pennsylvania, have banned the use of electronic and battery-powered duck decoys.

The Wonderduck and its fellow robotic decoys are just one example of the gadgets and gear available to the modern hunter that have resulted from technological innovation. The hunting gear of the twenty-first century is very different from that of even fifty years ago because technological advances in other sectors have been applied to hunting. Improvements in textiles have led to the development of lighter, warmer, and more durable fabrics that can protect a hunter from inclement weather and allow longer hunting trips in an expanded hunting season. The development of reliable all-terrain vehicles (ATVs) allows easier and faster transport of hunters deeper into wilderness areas and decreases the difficulties in transporting gear and animals. Satellites and Global Positioning System (GPS) units can be used to give a hunter both his current location and the location of his prey. Advances more directly related to hunting itself, are the technological alterations in rifles and other weapons that have increased the power, speed, and accuracy of hunters' shots. In addition to the more powerful weapons, the specialized scopes and sights that can be added to the weapons have taken hunters many steps above standard bows and arrows.

To many hunters, the changes in technology and gear are a natural part of man's innovation that increases the efficiency of hunting. Other hunters feel that the increased reliance on gadgets and technology has decreased the skill of hunters and taken the need to practice and become proficient away from hunting as a sport. Animal rights activists feel that the new technological advances give humans an unfair, unethical advantage over the animals they hunt. The underlying question remains: When is the use of new technology not only overkill, but also cheating because of the shortcuts it creates that negate the impact of skill, talent, and practice? The authors of the viewpoints in chapter 2 discuss the positive and negative impact of modern technological advances on hunting.

> *"The fact is, young adults and new hunters have no idea what it was like 20 years ago. So, how have things changed? Consider our gear."*

Technological Advances Can Improve Hunting Skills

Jim Zumbo

In this viewpoint, Jim Zumbo discusses the positive impact that technology has had on hunting. Zumbo notes that the many improvements in clothing, boots, optics, electronics, and rifles have improved hunting skills. Jim Zumbo is a lecturer, hunter, forester, and wildlife biologist, and he is the former hunting editor of Outdoor Life.

As you read, consider the following questions:

1. What is the difference between a "woods techie" and a traditional hunter, according to Zumbo?
2. What are some of the changes in clothing technology the author describes?
3. What electronic devices does Zumbo state are new to hunting over the past fifty years?

Last fall I walked up to a young hunter sitting on a log. He was fiddling with a GPS [Global Positioning System] unit, obviously puzzled. We struck up a conversation about the unit he was using. He was unsure of where he was and was confused by the GPS readings.

I grinned and asked if he had a compass. He looked up at me and said he didn't own one. He'd heard they were complicated.

I told him the direction he needed to go in and watched him walk off. He wore the latest camo [camouflage] design, a new binocular and new boots—all in all, a walking sporting-goods catalog. *There goes a real woods techie*, I thought. I suspected he had little hunting or outdoors savvy.

A Generation Gap

My earliest hunting mentors were my grandfather, my uncles and my dad. In those days we hunted on the outskirts of the city we lived in; today that area is occupied by housing developments, malls and other civilized structures. Practically all of us can relate to such changing times, but think for a minute about the new hunter.

A person born in 1985, ready to enter college now [in 2004] and looking to hunt, has never known a world without HIV/AIDS, or *The Tonight Show* without Jay Leno. Most have never seen a television without a remote control or a telephone without buttons. They don't know who shot J.R.[a television character from the 1980s]—they don't even know who J.R. was.

The fact is, young adults and new hunters have no idea what it was like 20 years ago. So, how have things changed? Consider our gear.

Gear That Improves the Hunting Experience

At the top of the list is camouflage clothing. Before the 1980s, the basic camo design was the military woodland pattern. Then came Trebark, soon followed by Realtree and Mossy

Technology Gives Hunters an Edge

"Yes, it's unbelievable how technology has given today's hunter an edge," said Jeff Jones of the Independence [Missouri] Dick's [Sporting Goods] store.

"With the new stealth cameras hunters have a better chance to see what's out there. . . .

"The new bows shoot faster and flatter. The new scent-lock clothing allows you to go completely undetected. The list of things you can get just goes on and on."

Gene Fox, "Technology Changes Hunter's Edge,"
[Eastern Jackson County, MO] Examiner,
October 15, 2003. www.examiner.net/stories.

Oak. Before long there were more than a dozen designs on the market. Camo clothing actually became a trendy fashion statement. Hunters wear it whether they're going hunting or not. It's the style in airports, in restaurants and even in hunting towers, where the fully clad camo hunter peers out of a small window, or more curiously still, where hunter orange is required to cover the camo. It doesn't matter; camouflage is the thing to wear.

I wear camouflage for a couple of reasons. Some of the garments are made of tough, waterproof fabric and have a sturdy hood and all sorts of deep pockets to accommodate my gear. I also wear camo for the purpose for which it's made—to hide from the quarry. I wear hunter orange for safety reasons when I'm hunting big game, but if I'm hunting turkeys, waterfowl or predators, I'll wear camouflage from my nose to my toes.

Fabric technology has made great strides. Wool was the material of choice many decades ago, and it still is in cold, damp weather. My wool clothing is always handy, and I especially appreciate it when I'm headed out into stormy mountains. But now there's Gore-Tex as well. Garments lined with Gore-Tex fabric are not only lightweight, but are waterproof as well (though the effectiveness can vary depending on the quality of the garment). Undergarments are now made from synthetic materials that we can hardly spell. Polypropylene, chloropropylene and others wick moisture away from our bodies and keep us warm and dry.

The latest rage among deer hunters is scent-blocking fabrics that incorporate charcoal filtration to mask human scent from a deer's sensitive nose.

Hunting boots have changed dramatically. I had to constantly massage my first boots with a homemade mixture that included bear grease to keep them waterproof, but today's boots require no such care. They also grip better and you can find tread designs for any hunting situation you might encounter. I prefer an air-bob sole, which in my experience handles slippery slopes better than any other design.

Optics have also gone through extraordinary changes in the last couple of decades. My first riflescope was a fixed four-power, and I did quite well with it for 20 years. In fact, it's still my favorite type of scope, but the 3-9X variable is the current darling among most hunters. Most noteworthy is the technology inside the scope. Nowadays there are all sorts of reticles and gizmos that help you judge a bullet's drop over a certain range, and some allow you to quickly figure how far away an animal is standing. That's not my cup of tea; I don't want to have to use my brain to interpret the little lines and circles in the scope when an elk is about to bust into the timber and I have just a moment to make the shot.

My idea of a great scope is one that is absolutely waterproof and fogproof and has a crisp focus, a simple crosshair with a dot in the middle and excellent light-gathering capability in low light. Ditto for the binocular (minus the crosshair, of course), but make mine roof prisms that won't break my neck after wearing them all day. The old Porro prisms that weighed 15 pounds (well—it seemed like it) are stored in my attic. Spotting scopes are the least-used hunting optic, but the most important in open-country situations. A couple dozen years ago you had to be totally sold on the spotting-scope concept because they were bulky and heavy. Today they're compact, light and a joy to use.

The range finder has become a big hit in the optics industry. Now we can confirm that an elk is indeed standing out there at 318 yards instead of 267 or 418. I think that's perfectly acceptable. Anything that helps us to make a more accurate shot is okay.

Rise of the Synthetic Stock

Guns haven't changed a whole lot if you look at their external features. What has changed dramatically in firearms is the disappearance of the once-beloved wood stock. My first serious big-game rifle was a Winchester Model 70, primarily because I was a devoted [gun writer] Jack O'Connor fan and this was his rifle of choice. If there were any synthetic stocks around in 1963 when I got this rifle, I didn't see them, but I would have considered it blasphemy to own any firearm that didn't have a wooden stock. I was proud of the nicks and scratches on that Winchester's stock after 20 years of use. Then something happened to my brain. I actually handled a gun with a synthetic stock, tried it and liked it. Now, synthetic stocks are my choice. They offer lighter weight and better accuracy and don't make me wince when they get scratched.

The Electronic Revolution

The electronic devices that are commonplace today simply didn't exist when I was starting to hunt. Now we can tell how many deer walk down a trail and even take pictures of them with a camera attached to a tree. Patterning is now the all-important strategy. When we kill a deer or elk, we can call our pals on a two-way radio and ask for help to get it out of the woods. Where we have cell phone service, we can call our wives, bosses or kids from the tree stand, and if we have a satellite phone we can make a call from the middle of the tundra above the Arctic Circle or from a Yucatan jungle. My biggest concern with any electronic equipment is ethics and fair chase. Hunters who use two-way radios to guide each other to game, for example, should be banished from the woods. Those who carry the new heat-seeking units designed to help find wounded deer should also hit the road if they attempt to use the devices to locate healthy, hidden animals.

Portable GPS units are marvelous. I haven't figured out how to use them yet, but if they allow you to penetrate the woods with more confidence and find more game, then go for it. But they do run on batteries. It's still good to keep a compass handy.

So what's ahead? I wish I could look into the crystal ball and say for sure, but since I can't, I'll say that we're in for more vastly improved electronic gear, profound advances in optics and perhaps a GPS unit that even I can figure out. But some things will never change. We still put our hunting pants on one leg at a time.

"If ever we become slaves to our technology, we can no longer call ourselves hunters."

Use of High-Tech Gadgets Diminishes Hunting Skills

Jim Carmichel

In this viewpoint, Jim Carmichel discusses the impact that recent advances in sporting technology have had on hunting. He discusses the possibility that advances in technology have taken the need for skill out of hunting and may now provide hunters an unfair advantage over wildlife. Jim Carmichel is the author of several books, shooting editor of Outdoor Life *magazine, and a firearms expert.*

As you read, consider the following questions:

1. What does Carmichel believe is the one overarching standard of ethical hunting and good sportsmanship that every hunter should follow?
2. What medieval weapon's invention does Carmichel say led to an ethical debate over the use of the item?

3. What is Carmichel's concern about the adoption of new imaging technology when hunting?

Will advances in technology take the "hunt" out of hunting?

The hunter wore neither blaze-orange nor camo [camouflage]; his hunting attire was a silken shirt with puffy sleeves and lace cuffs over which he wore a gold-embroidered jerkin of purple velvet. Crimson bows garnished his spool-heeled boots, and his face was framed by curly locks of sandy hair cascading to his shoulders. He carried no gun or bow, but in each of his doeskin-gloved hands was a long-bladed dagger.

He stood blocking the narrow escape route of a bunting-draped enclosure, and the object of his attention was a magnificently antlered stag, head held high, that was charging in his direction. Scattered beyond the enclosure were the bloody remains of similar stags that had apparently met their fate at the pointed tips of the hunter's keen blades. Also beyond the enclosure was a garlanded grandstand filled with gentlemen and ladies as richly dressed as the hunter himself. Their expressions and gestures signaled immense enthusiasm for his skill, while farther in the background even more deer were being driven forward by a circle of slack-faced peasants.

This scene was depicted in a painting I once saw in a London art gallery. On its frame an engraved brass plate read simply: "The Deer Park, English, Artist Unknown, circa 1600–1650."

Though we might be repelled by images of such gratuitous slaughter, we would do well to keep in mind that those were days of unrestrained and reckless virility, and the dandified hunter might have been equally appalled by the notion of killing deer with a firearm or bow.

What Is Fair?

That picture comes to mind when I see or hear about the latest in sporting technology. Scent-blocking hunting clothes, decoys with fluttering wings, portable tree stands, cartridges that shoot farther and rifle scopes that beam silent lasers to gauge distance. Great technology, sure, but at what juncture do we sacrifice sportsmanship for technoship? Or have we already crossed that bridge?

Whichever side our personal experiences and conscience dictate we take on this and similar issues, it behooves the thinking sportsman to contemplate the larger and universal concepts of sportsmanship.

Most of us view "good sportsmanship" as taking game or fish by means that are "fair." Is it fair to shoot a duck on the water, a pheasant on the ground or a dove on a limb? To snag a fish or bag a deer within a fenced enclosure? Do scope-sighted, in-line muzzleloaders and compound bows impinge unfairly on special hunting seasons intended for traditional blackpowder arms and bows? Do electronic fish finders take the "sport" out of sport-fishing? Just as it is mankind's unique gift to conceive, build and utilize such tools, we also possess the unique—and often troubling—gift of being able to evaluate our societal obligations and balance them against the benefits and hazards of such tools. Throughout history there have been many such reckonings.

One example that comes to mind is the introduction of the crossbow back in medieval times. So powerful was the belt from this infernal contraption that it could pierce the finest armor. Thus it was deemed decidedly un-Christian to employ such advanced technology against one's fellow Christians. It was perfectly acceptable, however, to use crossbows against any infidels that a Christian army might encounter.

Once, when I was bird shooting in the mountains of northern India, my host took me on a side trip to show off a trout-restocking program he and a group of his fellow sportsmen were promoting. What I remember best about that visit is the signs posted along the swiftly running stream, each of

A Low-Tech Approach

"Much of this stuff ranges from the totally irrelevant to the completely superfluous," says Jim Posewitz, who runs Orion, The Hunter's Institute, a nonprofit organization that lobbies for ethical and responsible hunting. "I'm a minimalist. The more honest the relationship, the better.

"To preserve hunting, you have to preserve the hunting ethic," says Posewitz, for 32 years a Montana game biologist. "If you have even a sliver of doubt, the advantage must go to the animal being hunted."

Candy Thomson, "Technology Has Ushered Hunting into More Sophisticated Season: Gizmos, Gadgets, Electronic Devices Now Drive Industry," Baltimore Sun, *November 26, 2006.*

them bearing a clever ditty besmirching the honor of fishermen who did not use artificial flies only.

Though I laud my host's efforts at establishing a trout fishery in those cold Himalayan waters, I have difficulty agreeing with him or any group who would impose their concept of fair play on others who, by tradition or necessity, hold quite different views of sportsmanship. Likewise my reaction to anyone questioning the use of technically advanced hunting tools—with certain reservations, which I'll come to later.

So, What Is Acceptable?

Using range-finding scopes as an example, their benefits are obvious when we take into consideration that range estimation is one of the very least reliable of all our learned hunting skills. At distances of up to 150 yards or thereabouts, we can usually come pretty close; farther out than that it's not uncommon for range estimates to be off by 100 yards or more, even by experienced hunters and guides.

To a greater degree than we're likely to admit, a big reason for the popularity of "flat-shooting" cartridges is that they tend to forgive poor range estimation. But with the 300-plus-yard "trophy" shots that increasing numbers of hunters are attempting, a more precise means of distance measuring is imperative. And I'm all for it, so long as hunters use the technically proved information wisely and are not tempted to try shots beyond the reach of their marksmanship or equipment.

Even when a hunter knows the exact distance to his target, he still must apply a skillful knowledge of his rifle's trajectory, how much to aim over or under the exact spot he wants his bullet to hit, how much to allow for crosswinds and, that most basic hunting skill of all, marksmanship.

Now let's consider the next generation of laser range-finding scopes, which I am certain will be on the market sooner rather than later—aiming devices that employ trajectory-compensating reticles (TCR)!

Yeah, sure, tricky multi-dot and mil-dot reticles that give us some idea of where to aim at different ranges have been around for ages, but a TCR aiming device is another species altogether. Notice I say "aiming device" rather than scope, because such instruments might have few optical components. They also might not look like the optical scopes we're used to, which won't matter all that much since lots of today's rifles don't look like rifles are supposed to look either.

The "eyepiece," as such, will be a screen similar to that of a digital camera, with the image of a reticle imposed thereon. The image of your target will be magnified electronically, and you will be able to take your pick of reticle options: crosshair, dot, post. The heart of the TCR aiming instrument will be a mini-computer that reads the distance input and adjusts the reticle so that it coincides with the position of the bullet at whatever distance the range finder is reading.

With the TCR instrument, you'd simply load the cartridge data into the device itself and it would go to work when its range finder told it the distance to your target. It could even be programmed to allow for wind drift.

The TCR, which represents a combination of existing technologies, is certainly intriguing. But would you go for it? Or would I? Probably not, because it only duplicates the skills that most hunters possess and proudly apply. But for future generations of hunters, hatched and nourished in technospheres, such equipment may seem to be as logical as a good compass and warm boots. If any of my pals should feel that such a device would make him a better, or at least more successful, hunter, I'd say go for it. He'd still be welcome to sit by my campfire and drink my whiskey.

Here Is the Line

Now let's look a bit further into the future and the possibility of a rifle-aiming gadget we'll call target-specific imaging (TSI). And don't think it's some Star Wars fantasy weapon, because the technology already exists in military sights.

In a sport-hunting version, the sight's computer will contain images of each animal—prairie dogs to pachyderms—from a variety of angles, and on each image there will be a designated optimal-aiming point. So when you aim at, say, a deer and pull the trigger, the sight's computer will flip through its images in a microsecond and find a match for the angle of the real deer you're shooting at. But even then the sight won't allow the rifle to fire until the reticle coincides with a specific optimal point of aim. You can't miss!

This level of technology has exciting and valuable military applications, but for sporting applications it reduces the rifle to a killing machine and the hunter to a mere accessory.

Which brings us back to my earlier suggestion, that we might surprise ourselves if we consider our personal views on sportsmanship and meld them with the sporting values of others.

I was faced with this reckoning years ago when I was shooting birds in an impoverished Asian province. The assistant assigned to me was a man who seemed to carry lightly the burdens of wife, children and hardship, yet could not comprehend my insistence on shooting birds on the wing. Shaking his head in wonderment, he opined, "Shoot them on the ground and you will get many more."

I remind myself of that incident whenever I find myself judging the sportsmanship of other hunters and their high-tech gear. But one thing I'm certain of is [that] if ever we become slaves to our technology, we can no longer call ourselves hunters.

> "Had this new [Internet hunting] tech-
> nology been available then, I would
> have been able to share one last hunt
> with [my father]; a memory that would
> be with him and with me today."

Internet Hunting Can Be a Useful Application of Technology for the Disabled

Steven Christian

In this viewpoint, Steven Christian discusses what he views as a positive role for Internet hunting. Christian asserts that Internet hunting can be conducted in an ethical manner for individuals with disabilities to allow them to hunt. However, the author notes that the technology should be tightly regulated to prevent misuse and abuse. Steven Christian is a hunter, an engineer, and past president of the Maryland Sportsmen's Association.

As you read, consider the following questions:

1. What situation does Christian describe that could result in a need for hunting over the Internet?

2. What does Christian feel hunters cherish the most about their experiences?

Steven Christian, "Internet Hunting II," *Hunter Alert!*, February 2006. http://mysite.verizon.net/mdhunteralert. Reproduced by permission.

3. Why might Homeland Security become involved in the issue of Internet hunting, according to Christian?

There was this guy I know that hunted all 'cross the US, Canada, Mexico, South America and even Africa. One day he was riding his ATV [all-terrain vehicle] and it rolled, with him on it, down a steep embankment. His friend, riding on another ATV, used his cell phone to call 911 because his friend was unable to move. They were in a remote woods and it took quite awhile for the paramedics to arrive on scene. After assessing the injured rider, they decided to call in a Medevac helicopter medical transport service to transport the injured person.

On arrival at the hospital's emergency trauma unit, they stabilized and discovered massive internal injuries to the spleen, ribs, head, neck and back. Once stabilized, and [after] having surgery, he was finally moved to a stepdown unit for intensive care until further assessment and other possible surgeries could be decided.

Sometime later, the final diagnosis was delivered—he was now a quadriplegic. An avid hunter just days earlier, in a matter of moments ... he lost the ability to participate in one of the most enjoyable activities of his life. Sure, he would always have the memories, but never again could he trek into the woods with the hope of taking venison for his freezer or enjoy the anticipation of his quarry coming within shooting range. Even if he could be helped into the woods and he could make the decision of whether to shoot or let the animal walk on by, he could not hold or even fire the rifle.

OK, you have hopefully read through this far, now bear with me a little longer. Along comes this injured man's friend that was riding ATVs with him on that fateful day. He has been studying how he could bring back the enjoyment of hunting to his friend. The injured man's friend is a computer

A Quadriplegic Man on Internet Hunting

For Dale Hagberg, a quadriplegic in Ligonier, Ind., Live-Shot [a computer-assisted remote hunting Web site] is the only way he can hunt after being paralyzed in a diving accident almost 18 years ago. The 38-year-old was an avid bear and deer hunter in his teens, but now is dependent on a ventilator and unable to sit up in a wheelchair for more than a few hours at a time once a week. He has used Lockwood's site about a dozen times to target shoot and four times to hunt but has yet to bag anything. He uses his mouth to manipulate a joystick that moves a remote camera to zoom in and out of the target area on the ranch in Texas and to aim. . . .

Hagberg said he understands the opposition to Internet hunting, but this is what he has to say to critics: "I think if they walked in my shoes for a while or knew someone like me, they'd feel differently."

Sylvia Moreno, "Mouse Click Brings Home Thrill of the Hunt,"
Washington Post, May 8, 2005, p. A01. www.washingtonpost.com/
wp-dyn/content/article/2005/05/07/AR2005050701270_pf.html.

Granted, the above is fictional (at least to me) but I know Medevac personnel that have seen similar trauma cases, my wife is a nurse in a trauma stepdown unit and it is a real and heart-wrenching experience for them. But to the injured person it now becomes a new way of life devoid of a large part of who he is. What is not fictional is the exact capability to take a person such as in the fictional story above on a hunt.

This scenario is not the norm for hunters, but the memories of our hunt and the feeling of anticipation and the ultimate decision at the moment of truth have not changed. After all, these are the things most hunters cherish about hunting.

The only thing missing above was physically being there—a medical and physical impossibility in the above case.

What is not fictional to me is the death of my own father. It was a slow lingering unwinnable battle with ALS [the progressive motor neuron disease Amyotroptic Lateral Sclerosis]. He was not an avid hunter but would always tell me that he would have liked to have gone on some of my hunts. Had this new technology been available then, I would have been able to share one last hunt with him—a memory that would be with him and with me today and to the day I die.

Now, how does all of this meld with the situation I find myself in today? The anti-hunting crowd has taken the possibility of the above fictional story and turned hunters' heads with screams of "animal cruelty" rhetoric and even invoked threats of terrorists from the use of such technology.

First off, I think the above scenario does not portray the visions of animal cruelty or even unfair hunting practices that some hunters are being misled to believe under the rules of Fair Chase.

Secondly, the smokescreen of terrorists using this technology feeds on fears that combine to further cast a black eye on hunters. That the Congressional Resolution (H.R. 1558) [a 2006 bill to prohibit computer-assisted remote hunting] is in the Committee on Homeland Security should tell you that technology will always be misused where it serves a military purpose. This technology is no different, but between you and me it has been around long before it was adapted to hunting; remember the film *Day of the Jackal*? Ask any military professional and they will tell you that similar technology has been in use for years; we have even seen it on the evening news.

But let me get back to the situation at hand.

Do I support the endeavor of the gentleman that started his business [Internet-based remote hunting] that opened up this whole can of worms? *No!* Why?, Because he is in it at a cost much higher than I think is reasonable, did not limit it to people such as I described above, and I don't think his heart is in the same place as mine. However, the free market has a way of setting a selling price that people are willing to pay and I don't think his price is going to keep him in business very long.

Do I support the adaptation of the technology for persons with afflictions, illnesses and disabilities that prevent them from continuing or even learning to hunt? *Yes!* I think I have already covered the why.

Do I support regulations on the use of this technology? *Yes!* This application of technology needs to be as tightly regulated as other hunting practices. Users of this technology should be certified on both sides of the screen; the person behind the mouse should have to meet stringent requirements from a medical standpoint, and the person behind the remotely activated rifle should have to meet stringent business and hunting guidelines.

Do I believe that the anti-hunting crowd would accept such regulations? *No way, no how!* Because it is not the technology they want to stop; it is hunting they want to stop—any way they can, and they seem to have blinded the vast majority of sportsmen into helping them. However, I will not be led down their path of misrepresentation and fear-mongering to support their overall agenda. I just hope that some sportsmen and proclaimed sportsmen's organizations come to their senses as well.

> *"Any managed situation manipulated to significantly reduce the animal's chance to survive is a canned hunt and therefore fails to meet the hunting community's own standard for hunting."*

Canned and Internet Hunting Are Ethically Wrong

The Humane Society of the United States

In this viewpoint, the Humane Society of the United States (HSUS) details the reasons that canned and other types of hunting that reduce the animal's chance of survival are immoral. The viewpoint details the animal protection advocate's view of canned hunting as an inhumane form of killing that violates fair chase principles. The HSUS is the nation's largest animal protection organization.

As you read, consider the following questions:

1. What is canned hunting, according to HSUS?
2. In the view of the HSUS, how is the concept of fair chase explained?

The Humane Society of the United States, "Canned Hunts: Unfair at Any Price, 4th edition," *Report by The Humane Society of the United States*, January 2005. Reproduced by permission of The Humane Society of the United States, humanesociety.org.

3. What does HSUS state are the four main elements of ethical hunting?

The closing decades of the twentieth century saw the rise of a new kind of "sport" in North America: the "canned hunt." Although canned hunts advertise under a variety of names—most frequently "hunting preserves," "game ranches," or "shooting preserves"—they can be identified by the two traits they all have in common: they charge their clients a fee to kill an animal; and they violate the generally accepted standards of the hunting community, which are based on the concept of "fair chase." In some cases animals may be shot in cages or within fenced enclosures; in others they may be shot over feeding stations. Some of the animals are tame and have little fear of humans, while others may be tied to a stake or drugged before they are shot. But whatever method is used, the defining characteristic of a canned hunt is that the odds have been artificially manipulated against the animal so heavily that the notion of fair chase is subverted. Canned hunts are commercial hunts that take place on private land under circumstances that virtually assure the hunter of success. . . .

The Reality of Canned Hunts

A sweltering summer day forces a large lion under the shade of a drooping tree amidst a bucolic landscape. She pants from the heat, unconcerned at the sight of an approaching man wearing a pristine white shirt and clean, khaki pants. He stops about 100 feet from the tree and animal. As the feline lies in the relaxing shade, the man raises a rifle pointed toward the drowsy animal. An unseen voice directs the lone gunman. He shoots once and the lion, wounded and disoriented, races from the shade of the tree. Only her cries of pain can be heard and her flailing limbs seen over the grass. The voice again directs the man to shoot again after seconds have elapsed as the creature struggles for life. The second shot finishes the job. The man nervously approaches the feline and butts her with his gun. He then gives thumbs-up to the camera, bends down and feels her coat. . . . The camera pans out to show a tall, chain-link fence. [CBS Morning News]

Although canned hunts are advertised as rugged, outdoor adventures, in reality they are conducted in an atmosphere of comfort and convenience. You can fly into a hunting preserve in the United States, and after a gourmet dinner, you can spend the night in a luxurious hunting lodge. The next day, you'll be given a high-powered rifle with a brief orientation to its use and driven to the "shooting area." The area is usually a fenced enclosure from which there is no escape, ranging from a few square yards to several hundred acres, depending on how strenuous you want your hunt to be.

The outcome is never really in doubt. In many cases, the hunting preserve will give a guarantee: "No kill, no pay." Whether the area is large or small, the animals are either fenced in—so that they cannot escape and have no hiding place that is secret from the guide—or they have been habituated to eating at a feeding station at the same time every day. At many ranches, the same truck that brings dinner to the feeding stations also brings the hunters. Exotic animals bought from breeders are often accustomed to people feeding them and cleaning their cages, so they have no fear of humans. They are often surplus zoo animals or retired circus performers who are too habituated to humans or too old and arthritic to run away.

The essentials are always the same regardless of the cost of the trip: an animal who is either fenced in, lured to feeding stations, or habituated to humans, and odds so heavily in the hunter's favor that there is little risk of leaving without a trophy. Most canned hunts have taxidermists on site or on call to mount your trophy, whose fate was sealed the moment you made your reservation. . . .

Internet Hunting Is Unsportsmanlike

Why any one person would need to use the global nature of the Internet to shoot an unsuspecting forest or jungle creature is a mystery to me. I'm not going to get into the morality of hunting. I know many consider it a sport, while others find it horrifying. But I'd be surprised if a sportsman in the mode of Ernest Hemingway would find any honor in bagging deer this way.

Lance Ulanoff, "Hunting Site Shoots Self in Foot,"
PC Magazine, *May 2005.*

Ethical Objections

Trophy hunting is a sport whose object is to kill sentient beings for pleasure, and that can never be ethical. It is a sport in which only the aggressor participates willingly; the victim has no choice in the matter. And it is a sport in which the stakes are dreadfully uneven—if the animal loses, he or she dies; if the hunter loses, he or she goes home empty-handed and life goes on as before. That being said, we all recognize that among ethically objectionable acts, some are more heinous than others. Due to their egregious brutality and blatant violation of the hunting community's "fair chase" standard, canned hunts inspire a higher level of outrage than more traditional forms of hunting, even to the extent that many staunch defenders of sport hunting are vocal opponents of canned hunts.

Hunting advocates defend the ethics of their sport by invoking the concept of "fair chase." Even the protrophy hunting Safari Club International has a code of ethics in which the hunter pledges "to comply with all game laws in the spirit of fair chase, and to influence my companions accordingly." "Fair chase" is left undefined. In an affidavit for hunters who wish to have a trophy buck recorded in its record books, the Boone and Crockett Club (B&C) defines fair chase as "the ethical, sportsmanlike, and lawful pursuit and taking of any free-ranging, wild, native North American big game animal in a manner that does not give the hunter an improper advantage over such game animals." This statement leaves several key terms, including "ethical," "sportsmanlike," and "improper advantage" undefined, although B&C does give examples of practices that violate fair chase, such as shooting an animal who is helpless when mired in deep snow or swimming in the water.

Defining Hunting Ethics

Jim Posewitz spent 32 years as a biologist with the Montana Department of Fish, Wildlife, and Parks. As founder and president of Orion: The Hunter's Institute, he is one of sport hunting's most passionate defenders, much in demand as a speaker by hunting organizations and wildlife agencies across the country. In his book, *Beyond Fair Chase*, which is widely viewed within the hunting community as the "bible" of hunting, Posewitz discusses fair chase in these terms: "Fundamental to ethical hunting is the idea of fair chase. This concept addresses the balance between the hunter and the hunted. It is a balance that allows hunters to occasionally succeed while animals generally avoid being taken." One page later, he notes that, "The concept of fair chase is important to hunting. The general public will not tolerate hunting under any other circumstances." Posewitz's organization, Orion, defines hunting as "the fair chase pursuit of free-roaming wildlife in a noncompetitive situation in which the animal is used for food."

Orion's definition of ethical hunting includes four elements: 1) fair chase; 2) free-roaming wildlife; 3) noncompetitive; and 4) used for food. The first two elements are shared with the definition used by B&C. Since B&C exists to promote trophy hunting, its definition of fair chase does not include "a noncompetitive situation" or consuming the animal.

Fair chase is the fundamental standard put forward by defenders of hunting. All other defenses of hunting for sport depend on and derive from the notion of fair chase. But hunting on game ranches and preserves is killing for fun and bragging rights under circumstances in which the traditional defenses of hunting become meaningless. And as we have already seen, such hunting makes a mockery of the alleged ethical codes of the hunting community. Therefore, is hunting on game ranches and hunting preserves really hunting at all, or is it something else entirely—something quite different that is masquerading as hunting?

Outdoor writer Ted Kerasote, whose popular book, *Bloodties: Nature, Culture, and the Hunt,* is an impassioned defense of hunting, including trophy hunting, has no doubt about the answer to this question: "Wildlife is not livestock. The problem comes when people are supposedly hunting these animals. That's the problem right there." According to Kerasote, canned hunts are turning hunting "into this caged, paid affair and it bears no resemblance to what hunting is, was, and could be. Like so many things in our world, people want to buy the product (the trophy) rather than experience the process (meeting the animal on its own terrain)."

Orion's definition of "ethical" hunting and Kerasote's comments provide an excellent standard for identifying canned hunts and making judgments about them by comparison to traditional hunting. *And these judgments will not be made according to the standards of the animal protection community, but according to the standards of the hunting community.* In fact, we can conclude from both Orion and B&C's definitions that any managed situation manipulated to significantly reduce the animal's chance to survive is a canned hunt and therefore fails to meet the hunting community's own standard for hunting. . . .

An Animal Advocate's View

In August 1995, The Fund for Animals' former national director, Heidi Prescott (now The Humane Society of the United States' senior vice president of campaigns), was invited to speak at the Fourth Annual Governor's Symposium on North America's Hunting Heritage in Green Bay, Wisconsin. It may seem implausible to have an animal protection advocate speaking to a conference of the hunting community's leaders; her speech, however, entitled "How Hunters Make My Job Easy," challenged hunters to clean up their own ranks and speak out against egregious practices such as canned hunts. She asked:

> What do people who may not have strong feelings about hunting either way . . . [think when they read] in their local newspaper about someone paying thousands of dollars to kill a tame lion or sheep on a fenced-in ranch? . . . Do you think that the average person who looks at this practice thinks that hunting is a spiritual outdoor experience, and that hunters respect the wild and are the great wildlife managers and conservationists they claim to be? I can tell you what they think, because they call The Fund for Animals' office to express their horror, their sorrow, and ask what they can do to help.

The Fund for Animals and The Humane Society of the United States are committed to working with hunters and state wildlife agency officials—people with whom we may never agree on many issues—to find areas where we have common ground and common interests. We believe that the issue of canned hunts is one of those areas. To animal protection advocates, a canned hunt is the inhumane killing of an animal simply for a trophy. To hunters, a canned hunt is a violation of the fair chase standard and a blight on the image of their sport. To biologists, a canned hunt is a time bomb of potential disease for native wildlife populations.

All in all, it would be difficult to find anyone who would be willing to defend canned hunts—except, perhaps, the operators who profit by breeding or trading in animals who are marked as guaranteed trophies and the hunters who lack the skill or the inclination to hunt in the wild.

Periodical Bibliography

The following articles have been selected to supplement the diverse views presented in this chapter.

Jeff Barnard — "Technology Pushes Envelope of Hunting," *ESPN.com.*, originally posted March 23, 2005, updated June 6, 2005. www.sports.espn.go.com.

Eric Goldman — "A Website for Hunting Poses Questions About Killing," *San Jose Mercury News*, July 25, 2005.

David Hart — "Bolt from the Blue," *Outdoor America*, undated. www.iwla.org.

Robert MacMillan — "This Mouse Won't Hunt," *WashingtonPost.com*, April 23, 2005. www.washingtonpost.com.

Chris Madson — "A Matter of Spin," *Wildfowl*, 2007. www.wildfowlmag.com/conservation/WF0509_con.

Kevin McDermott — "Bill Would Ban Remote-Controlled Hunting," *St. Louis Post-Dispatch*, January 22, 2007.

Eric Sharp — "Video Sight Is the Next Big Thing in Hunting Technology," *Detroit Free Press*, February 9, 2005.

Christopher Stern — "Hunters in a Hurray Embrace Advanced Gadgets in the Field," *Washington Post*, January 3, 2004.

Candy Thomson — "Technology Has Ushered Hunting into More Sophisticated Season: Gizmos, Gadgets, Electronic Devices Now Drive Industry," *Baltimore Sun*, November 26, 2006.

Bonnie Tsui — "Trophies in a Barrel: Examining 'Canned Hunting'" *New York Times*, April 9, 2006.

Steve Wright — "New Technology in Clothing Makes Hunting Easier, or at Least More Comfortable," *ESPNOutdoors.com*, January 13, 2007. http://sports.espn.go.com/outdoors.

CHAPTER 3

Is Hunting an Important Part of Wildlife Maintenance?

Chapter Preface

In a suburb of Detroit, a woman sitting on her back porch has a disturbing encounter with wildlife: A coyote runs by carrying her dead cat in its mouth. In a community forest, a wildlife management program leads to a large deer population that eats all of an endangered fern's tender shoots, causing other plants to take over the fern's biological niche. These scenes emphasize issues that arise when modern humans intersect with the natural world and soon need to develop effective solutions to solve the conflict between human and animal agendas. Communities addressing this clash frequently find that there are several possible solutions to their situation, and each is vigorously supported by members on both sides. As an example, in the scenes described above, some communities would choose a conservation plan that would consist of hiring hunters to reduce the coyote and deer populations by killing a certain number of animals. This solution would mainly be favored by hunters within the community. Other communities might choose a conservation plan that results in a trap-and-relocate program that would move spare animals to a new location. This solution would likely be favored by animal rights activists. Each of these solutions has one main underlying question that leads to debates: How do modern humans strike a reasonable balance among the expansion of urban and suburban human settlements, the conservation of wildlife, and the preservation of rural areas?

Since the 1920s, hunters have been faced with this dilemma of balance. As a group, they began addressing the issue by offering financial and legislative support of land conservation and wildlife management efforts. The most famous example of this is that of prominent hunter and U.S president Theodore Roosevelt's creation of a system of protected national parks, national forests, game and bird preserves, and other federal nature areas. Opponents of hunting, however, suggest a conflict of interest arises when hunters are linked to conservation and wildlife management. Hunters may wish to increase the number of female deer in a national forest so that during doe-hunting season there are more deer to shoot. In the long run, the hunter-championed increase in female deer could disrupt the natural interaction of the deer herd, lead to an overgrowth in the deer population, and disrupt the forest's ecosystem. Opponents of hunting are also more generally against community conservation plans that include the killing of animals by hunters to control population numbers in suburban and rural areas.

The debate between hunters and their opponents often centers on the rights of animals versus the rights of humans. Hunters following the rules of fair chase often believe that they are respecting basic animal rights by not taking an unfair advantage over animals while hunting. They feel that their efforts to conserve wilderness areas and animal populations are also supporting animals. Opponents of hunting say the bottom-line is that hunters wish to kill animals for sport. Hunting opponents feel that this underlying interest violates an animal's right to life, negates the positive effects of hunter-driven conservation efforts, and taints all such conservation plans with ulterior motives. This debate between hunters and their opponents is addressed in chapter 3 as each side discusses a central question: "Is hunting an important part of the conservation effort?"

"Until the politics of deer management change . . . [forest] researchers will be documenting an ongoing catastrophe rather than finding a practical solution to the problem."

Hunting Plays a Crucial Role in Maintaining Natural Habitats and the Environment

Sharon Levy

In this viewpoint, Sharon Levy discusses the need for hunting to manage the large deer population. Only through hunting will forest diversity be preserved, because the deer destroy many plants and animals through overgrazing. However, instead of the current model of hunting that lobbies for a continually increasing deer population, a revised hunting model is required to preserve natural forest habitat. Sharon Levy is a freelance writer based in California. This article has been revised or modified from the original.

As you read, consider the following questions:

    1. What change in the environment does Levy say led to an explosion in the deer population?

Sharon Levy, "A Plague of Deer," *Bioscience*, vol. 56, no. 9, September 2006, pp. 718–21. Republished with permission of the American Institute of Biological Sciences.

2. How has Yellowstone National Park created an increase in plant and animal diversity, according to Levy?

3. In Levy's view, what natural predator should hunters be imitating to most effectively decrease the deer population?

On the crest of a tall boulder grows a wild garden, bright with the blooms of trillium, mayflower, and Solomon's seal, and shaded by maple, birch, and hemlock trees. The plant life sheltering high on this rock in Pennsylvania's Allegheny National Forest (ANF) is a relic of the long-gone woodlands that once blanketed much of the eastern United States. Today such boulders, which are among the few spots that can't be reached by hungry deer, are diverse islands in a sea of monotony.

A Loss of Diversity

Much of the ANF is now dominated by black cherry trees, and the forest floor is covered in a thick mat of hay-scented fern. Both species have been part of the eastern woods for millennia. Now, because deer can't eat them, they've come to overwhelm nearly all their natural competitors. They are among the few successful survivors of a devastating plague of deer.

"The whole eastern US has been over-browsed for many decades," says Walter Carson of the University of Pittsburgh, who with his students and colleagues has been using the plant refuges on boulder tops to gauge the impact of deer in the ANF. Uncontrolled deer populations, he says, have collapsed the diversity of the forest. The only surviving plants are shade tolerant and are either unpalatable to deer or able to regrow quickly after browsing.

Loss of Predators and Prey

Pennsylvania is the state most severely affected by the problem, which began in the early 20th century, when wolves and cougars had been hunted to extinction in the east. Their one-time prey, the white-tailed deer, were facing the same fate. "It reached the point," Carson says, "where just seeing a deer rated a mention in a small town newspaper." So the Pennsylvania Game Commission brought in deer from Virginia and Wisconsin and put a moratorium on hunting those without antlers.

A Change in Vegetation

At the same time, forests across much of the Northeast were being clear-cut, a process that in Pennsylvania was completed by the mid-1930s. As any deer hunter knows, deer love a clear-cut. The new shrubs and grass that spring up in forest openings provide abundant browse. The deer population skyrocketed, and although limited hunting focused on bucks was reinstated, by the 1940s deer were radically changing eastern forests.

The hay-scented fern, for example, once covered less than 3 percent of the forest floor. Now, because it thrives in clear-cuts and deer devour its competitors, it dominates more than a third of the forested area in Pennsylvania and is abundant throughout much of the northeastern United States. Across more than half of the ANF, a carpet of hay-scented fern suppresses the growth of other native herbs and of tree seedlings in the understory. "If all the deer disappeared tomorrow," says Carson, "that dense layer of fern would continue to suppress the growth of new trees." In a recent review published in the *Canadian Journal of Forestry*, Carson and Alejandro Royo examined the formation of such "recalcitrant understory layers" worldwide. A similar pattern of logging and overbrowsing is affecting forests from New Zealand to Europe to North America. Some Pennsylvania clear-cuts where thick growths of fern and grass have taken hold remain empty of new trees 80 years after they were logged.

Understory plants are also hard hit. In a study published in *Science* in February 2005, James McGraw and Mary Ann Furedi of West Virginia University found that wild ginseng, a native herb that has long been collected for export to Asia, is being decimated by deer. Ginseng populations and individual plants have grown progressively smaller over the last century, and the harvest has shrunk by a factor of three or four since the 1800s.

In the field, Furedi soon learned to identify plants that had been browsed: They showed a distinctive tear on the stem, and telltale deer tracks or scat were often nearby. A browsed plant won't regrow until the following year, and it will come back smaller, producing fewer flowers and seeds. Based on a survey of 36 ginseng populations spread across eight states, McGraw and Furedi conclude that the species is on the brink of extinction. Most remaining populations are small, worsening the odds of survival. According to McGraw and Furedi's model, even the largest population, comprising 406 plants, has only a 57 percent chance of surviving this century.

"Ginseng is not particularly targeted by deer," says McGraw. "Deer eat it along with many other forest herbs. Trillium species, for instance, are heavily browsed by deer, with similar demographic consequences. I'm concerned that deer overpopulation will result in a desertification of the forest understory as herbaceous plants become fewer and less diverse."

The Impact of Overpopulation

The impacts of overpopulated deer on plants cascade through whole ecosystems: They've been shown to cause declines in the abundance and diversity of all kinds of forest creatures, from insects to mice to canopy-nesting birds. Perhaps the most dramatic illustrations of the power of deer to overwhelm an ecosystem come from Quebec's Anticosti Island, a landscape that had been empty of deer until 1896, when about 220 of them were brought there. The island's deer population boomed in the late 1920s, probably reaching more than 150,000. Aerial surveys since the late 1960s have produced population estimates ranging from 60,000 to 120,000 deer on the island's 7,943 square kilometers [3,067 square miles].

When Jean-Pierre Tremblay of the Université Laval recently revisited a series of Anticosti study sites that had been sampled in the 1970s, he was startled to find that deer numbers remain high, although the shrubs that deer prefer to eat had completely disappeared. The animals had been eating balsam fir, ordinarily, a food of last resort, taken only in times of starvation. Every fir seedling within reach of a deer had been devoured. The browsing pressure on balsam fir was so intense that the forest was shifting, being taken over by white spruce, which deer cannot eat at all.

Yet the deer endured. Tremblay discovered that they were feeding on balsam fir twigs, along with lichens, that fall out of the forest canopy during winter storms. This manna from above won't last forever, he says. "As the balsam fir forests become mature and die, they are replaced by white spruce that do not offer food for deer. But before starvation reduces the deer population, damage to the native forest occurs that may be difficult to reverse."

Other recent studies on Anticosti reveal deer as creatures that hold power most people may never have imagined. Steeve Côté, also of the Université Laval in Quebec, has documented the disappearance of both berry-producing shrubs and black bears on Anticosti Island since the arrival of deer. Black bears were once abundant there and fattened on a cornucopia of native berries in fall, allowing them to survive their winter hibernation. But during the first half of the 20th century, as deer browsed shrubs into oblivion, bear became rare and finally vanished altogether. The island has no alternative fall

Hunters Support Wildlife Maintenance

So why do I say hunters are good for the environment? Because the hunting community speaks out and pays out to ensure that wildlife populations of game species are sustainable from one generation to the next. This requires that a diversity of natural habitats be kept intact, unpolluted, and undisturbed. Hunters support these efforts with their attitudes about natural habitats and with their pocketbooks.

Whit Gibbons,
"Declining Hunters Still Good for the Environment," Ecoviews,
November 13, 2005. www.uga.edu/srel/ecoview11-13-05.htm.

food source that can sustain a bear population through the winter. Côté believes this is the first recorded instance of a large carnivore being extirpated by introduced herbivore.

The Role of Hunting

Deer hunting is the basis of Anticosti Island's economy; people living there have no wish to purge their home of introduced deer. Yet the deer, in the absence of efficient predators, are creating a plant community hostile to their own survival. Even if Anticosti is to be managed as a large deer farm, the numbers of deer must be reduced.

As early as the 1940s, Aldo Leopold, one of the founders of the conservation movement, was documenting the impacts of the human-engineered explosion of deer numbers. He recognized what was happening as a disaster, one that he and other wildlife managers who participated in the snuffing out of wolves and cougars had helped to create. He described the moment of this realization in his famous essay *Thinking Like A Mountain*:

We reached the old wolf in time to watch a fierce green fire dying in her eyes. . . . I was young then, and full of trigger-itch; I thought that because fewer wolves meant more deer, that no wolves would mean hunters' paradise. But after seeing the green fire die, I sensed that neither the wolf nor the mountain agreed with such a view. Since then, I have lived to see state after state extirpate its wolves. I have watched the face of many a newly wolfless mountain, and seen the south-facing slopes wrinkle with a maze of new deer trails. I have seen every edible bush and seedling browsed, first to anaemic desuetude, and then to death.

Managing the Hunt: A Cautionary Tale

Over the past 15 years, a wave of new studies has documented a renaissance of plant and animal diversity in Yellowstone National Park following the reintroduction of wolves there in 1995. The top dogs are affecting both the behavior and number of elk in the park, making possible a rebirth of aspen, willow, and other plants that were heavily browsed before.

Leopold's home state of Wisconsin now has its own small wolf population—about 400 animals, descendants of pioneers who made their way back from Minnesota and Michigan, without human assistance, decades after the species had been extirpated farther south. Don Waller of the University of Wisconsin-Madison is working with Wisconsin Department of Natural Resources biologists to measure the effect of the wolf's return: Their data show that where wolves live, the impacts of deer on cedar forests are being mitigated. But most of the state, like the majority of the areas in the eastern United States now heavily affected by deer overpopulation, is not wild enough to allow wolves to survive.

"Deer are changing plant communities dramatically," says Waller. "They eliminate seedlings of hemlock, cedar, and yellow birch and devour most understory plants with conspicuous flowers and fruits." In the wake of overbrowsing, grasses, sedges, and balsam fir have become dominant in Wisconsin forests. As in Pennsylvania and Quebec, these changes may be difficult or impossible to reverse.

The best way to control burgeoning numbers of deer, says Waller, is to get people to hunt more like wolves. "We should be shooting does, not bucks," he says. "We should have longer hunting seasons and ask hunters to shoot more than one deer." This kind of approach has been working well on Indian reservations in Wisconsin, which set their own hunting policies, and where hunters focus more on subsistence than on bagging a buck with an impressive rack. But for many hunters, the whole idea of shooting does clashes with traditions that go back to the early 20th century.

A Change in Management

Back then, when deer in Wisconsin and most of the eastern United States were recovering from near-extirpation, a brief hunt focused only on bucks made sense. But a century later, this kind of management appears deeply flawed. Changing the pattern is an uphill struggle. Some hunter groups continue to believe that the more deer, the better. They refuse to acknowledge the negative impacts of uncontrolled deer numbers, which include an increase in deer-related car accidents and a growing incidence of Lyme disease, in addition to the devastating effects on forests.

An influential minority of Pennsylvania hunters has stymied efforts to change deer management there. "We now have several generations of deer hunters who've grown up with deer at 40 to 60 animals per square mile," says Carson. "The advocates for keeping deer populations well above sustainable levels are incredibly vocal, well organized, and they win every time." The Pennsylvania Game Commission is controlled not by biologists but by deer hunters, whose license fees provide virtually all the commission's funding. "They think of deer as you would soybeans—the game commission should produce a lot of it," Carson observes.

Gary Alt, former chief deer biologist for the Pennsylvania Game Commission, tried to change hunting practices. In 1999,

Alt, who had worked as the commission's bear biologist for years, was given a new job: fixing the state's deer overpopulation problem. He increased the harvest of does and restricted shooting of bucks, a strategy designed to lower the overall numbers of deer while increasing the availability of large adult bucks most prized by hunters. The new management tactics began to work—but Alt resigned from his job in December 2004, after it became clear that the commissioners, under intense political pressure, were not going to let him stay the course. Although many hunters supported Alt, some who believe with fundamentalist fervor in their right to abundant deer complained loudly that prey were becoming harder to find.

Alt, who has received awards from the Pennsylvania Wildlife Federation, Audubon Pennsylvania, Safari Club International and the Quality Deer Management Association for his skills as a public educator, believes that while spreading the word about the realities of overpopulated deer herds is important, it is not enough. Wildlife management agencies like the Pennsylvania Game Commission should be funded by public money, not just by hunters, so that everyone with a stake in the future of forests and wildlife will have a meaningful say in their policies.

Until the politics of deer management change, say biologists like Alt, Waller, and Carson, researchers will be documenting an ongoing catastrophe rather than finding practical solutions to the problem.

> *"Far from being 'conservation' game management plans are destructive to the environment, ecology, biology and even certain businesses."*

Hunting Is Destructive to the Environment, Ecology, and Biology

Anne Muller, Interview by Yong Chau

In this viewpoint, Yong Chau discusses the relationship between conservation and hunting with Anne Muller, president of the Committee to Abolish Sport Hunting (CASH). The interview focuses on the destabilization of animal populations and the environment by hunting and hunting-supported wildlife-management programs. Yong Chau is a high school student who researched, interviewed, and created a Web page on the debate over sport hunting as part of an academic ThinkQuest team.

As you read, consider the following questions:

1. In what ways do hunters and hunter-supported wildlife-management programs increase the deer population, according to Muller?

Yong Chau, "Interview with Anne Muller, President of the Committee to Abolish Sport Hunting," *www.tqnyc.org*, 2006. Reproduced by permission.

2. How does the management of the deer population to ensure good trophy hunting affect the deer population, according to this viewpoint?

3. How does Quality Deer Management differ from Quantity Deer Management, in Muller's opinion?

Yong Chau: Many deer hunters say that they are conservationists and that deer hunting is good for the environment, good for stabilizing the deer population and necessary to keep deer from destroying woodlands. How would you respond to this?

Anne Muller: Sadly, deer populations are intentionally increased by wildlife managers in order to provide sport hunters with living targets. They increase populations in two ways:

First, they manipulate habitat to increase deer shelter and browse (deer food). Deer populations are naturally low in dense forest because there is little for deer to eat. By removing trees and thinning them out, or doing "controlled burns" the sun can hit the forest floor allowing more deer browse to grow.

Secondly, they manipulate the sex ratio between male and female deer, and skew the natural ratio (one male to one female) in favor of females. How do they do that? They permit hunters to take bucks only in many places. By reducing the male population they leave more browse for the females. Deer are polygamous and one male can impregnate many females. There is another phenomenon that kicks in after hunting season called "compensatory rebound." That occurs when the population is suddenly and drastically reduced, the remaining animals will have more offspring. Wildlife managers know that compensatory rebound in combination with bucks-only hunting ensures a high population in the autumn.

Quality Versus Quantity

There is a new form of management being done now: To accommodate the hunter demand for "trophy bucks," managers are trying to grow bucks with huge antlers for trophy hunting. That necessitates killing more females to allow the males to mature to the size that trophy hunters want to kill. So when you see regulations that allow for the taking of more females than males, or taking males with certain sized antlers, you will know that they are doing "Quality Deer Management" rather than "Quantity Deer Management." Quality deer management is much newer and is not as popular with hunters as being allowed to kill bucks without having to think about how large the racks are.

Deer and other popular game species (Canada geese, wild turkeys) are managed for high numbers at the expense of the 99% of the other species. That's not to mention that they are managed without respect for the residents or commercial orchards. Far from being "conservation" this is destructive to the environment, ecology, biology and even certain businesses.

So what you are saying is that hunting and conservation are complete opposites?

Exactly.

Canned hunting is legal in New York State [NYS]. Why is it legal when it is so cruel and so indulgent?

Actually, thanks to the animal rights movement, both the Senate and Assembly of the NYS legislature voted overwhelmingly to ban canned hunting. Governor [George] Pataki vetoed the bills! We heard that he did that for the farmers and those who profit from canned hunting operations.

What percentage of hunters are male and what percentage are female?

The last I looked, only 9% of hunters were female.

Do you think that hunters are more violent than non-hunters? Explain.

If you take a look at the kids who were involved in committing school massacres, it is clear that most were either young hunters or from families that hunted and had access to "sporting" firearms.

Hunters Show No Love for Wildlife

It is outlandish to hear sport hunters assert their sensitive side by proclaiming a "love" for wildlife. Their perverse definition of "love" allows for the stalking, terrorizing, and destruction of unsuspecting victims. Based upon this depraved standard, it could be reasonably argued that serial rapists love women and pedophiles love children. Would that somehow make these heinous violations any less repulsive?

Laura M. Nirenberg,
"Sport Hunting and the Humane Treatment of Animals?"
Animals Voice, *April 2005. www.animalsvoice.com/PAGES/writes/*
editorial/news/comment/hunting_humane.html.

Do you want to ban hunting totally? Explain why.

Yes, we want to ban hunting totally and wildlife management for hunting. We feel that it is environmentally destructive—as discussed above—in addition to being extremely cruel. Deer are not managed for the few people who claim to be subsistence hunters: they are managed for sport hunters. Simply because someone claims to eat what s/he kills does not qualify him or her as a subsistence hunter. Further, according to NRA [National Rifle Association] statistics, less than 1% of hunters actually eat what they kill.

Trapping is also considered part of hunting. A couple of months ago [in December 2005] a woman was walking her dog in a state park in the Hamptons and her dog was killed by a trap that was set right off the trail. What is your opinion of trapping and why is it allowed in public parks?

Recreational trapping is also an abomination. Animals suffer horribly in traps, and when someone traps to sell the fur, there are so many animals that are caught that have to be discarded because they are not the "right" animal. Trappers have bragged in their own publications when they have trapped an animal with only three legs (because it means that the animal had previously gotten away from another trapper by chewing off his leg). As you pointed out dogs and cats are caught in traps as traps are totally indiscriminate.

[In 2006], thanks to the animal rights movement, there is a bill pending in the NYS Legislature (A01835) that would give municipalities the ability to pass their own trapping restrictions or bans. Without the law, it's illegal for counties or towns to protect their citizens and companion animals or wildlife. *You can help* to pass the law. Please see www.humane voters.org and the link to "issues" for more information. We need you and your students to register your concern for the bill's passage ASAP!!

If people didn't hunt, wouldn't the earth become overpopulated with animals? Explain why you feel that way.

Not at all! Wildlife populations are self-regulating based on shelter, food supply, and disease. When we talk about overpopulation, we have to look at two types: biological and social. Most "overpopulation" that we hear about is socially perceived by some individuals complaining that there are too many of this or that. That's social perception. There are always intelligent, humane, and non-lethal methods of dissuading animals from where they are not wanted. Please keep in mind that management for game species keeps numbers artificially high.

Hunters accuse animal rights activists of being crazy. They say that you are even against killing cockroaches and vermin like rats. Can you explain if this is true or not?

What hunters say is clearly self-serving and tainted by their inability to understand that killing is wrong. It's like pedophiles who accuse their accusers of not understanding that there's nothing wrong with their behavior. We consider sport hunting to be that perverse. Yes, there are some people who oppose killing any creature, and why would we when there are other ways of dealing with the problem? For example, there are now plug-in high frequency sounds to keep mice and cockroaches away.

What can people who are against hunting do to stop hunting?

They can join our organization, stay in touch with our website www.all-creatures.org.cash, and especially join the League of Humane Voters [LOHV]. If you are in NYC [New York City] you can join www.humanenyc.org, and you can also join www.humanevoters.org.

Are there any other points you would like to add?

Just that the questions were very good. I wish I had the time to answer in more depth, but much of what I have said here is on our website: www.all-creatures.org/cash. Also, please stay in touch with the LOHV chapters, because legislation to stop hunting and trapping is really all that will stop it.

> "While [hunters and conservation groups] may not see eye-to-eye on every issue, what connects them is an understanding that healthy ecosystems mean healthy habitats for game animals."

Hunting Makes Significant Contributions to Wildlife Protections

Hal Herring

In this viewpoint, Hal Herring discusses the cooperative partnership between hunters and conservation groups to preserve wildlife and their habitat. Herring discusses the history of partnership starting with Theodore Roosevelt in the late nineteenth century and continuing into present-day collaborations between sporting and conservation groups. Hal Herring is a contributing editor at Field & Stream *and editor at large at* New West, *an Internet publication covering the Rocky Mountains and Western plains.*

As you read, consider the following questions:

1. What is one of the oldest forms of environmental advocacy, according to this viewpoint?

Hal Herring, "Today's Sportsmen and Sportswomen Are a Powerful Force for Conservation," *Nature Conservancy Magazine*, Autumn 2006. Reproduced by permission of the author.

2. How did the federal government support wildlife conservation in the 1930s, according to Herring?

3. In Herring's view, despite their partnership, on which issues do conservationists and hunters continue to disagree?

When a hunter dreams of a trophy elk, thoughts run to frozen mornings deep in the Rocky Mountains. Minnesota seldom comes to mind, and there's little reason why it should, since the state issued only five permits to hunt elk last year. Nonetheless, when The Nature Conservancy [a leading conservation organization] needed help acquiring a critical 800-acre piece of Minnesota grassland, it was the hunters of the Rocky Mountain Elk Foundation, based in faraway Montana, who stepped up.

Hunters and Conservation

Like a large percentage of the other 37.8 million hunters and anglers in the United States, the 150,000 members of the Rocky Mountain Elk Foundation are a powerful force for conservation, albeit one that is often misunderstood by nonhunters.

To be sure, many members of the self-described hook-and-bullet community don't look like stereotypical environmentalists. It's no secret, and no wonder, that hunters and nonhunting environmentalists often make each other nervous.

But what may come as a surprise is that sporting and conservation groups, including the Conservancy, frequently turn to each other as partners. And while they may not see eye-to-eye on every issue, what connects them is an understanding that healthy ecosystems mean healthy habitats for game animals.

"Different groups come to the same landscapes for different reasons and at times with different motivations," says Tom Cassidy, the Conservancy's director of federal programs, but "we have a common objective of conserving habitat." He adds: "I can't imagine not working with hunters and anglers—our shared values are too great."

"People who don't hunt should recognize that the motive of the hunters we work with is not simply to increase the numbers of animals for hunting, or even to have more places to hunt," says Matt Miller, a lifelong hunter who works for the Conservancy in Idaho. "It is a much bigger view of the land and the wildlife. I think of [late Sierra Club leader] David Brower. He loved to climb mountains, but he didn't work to preserve the mountains just so he'd have a nice place to climb."

Bart Semcer, a longtime hunter who works on fish and wildlife policy for the Sierra Club, emphasizes the importance of such partnerships: "Sportsmen are the original conservationists. You cannot do it without them."

The Original Conservationists

The idea that hunters are responsible for providing habitat for the game they hunt, and for the ecosystems that support game and other wildlife, is one of the oldest forms of environmental advocacy in North America, owing its existence to men like Theodore Roosevelt. Born in 1858, Roosevelt grew up steeped in the lore of Western hunting and adventure. But by the time he went west to hunt big game in 1883, he rode on horseback for 10 days across the grasslands of North Dakota before finding a bison to shoot. Roosevelt felt keenly the loss of a legacy that he believed had belonged to all Americans. He also saw, in the ruin of wildlife, the potential ruin of the nation.

When Roosevelt became president, he enacted the most sweeping environmental legislation the world had ever seen. "When he entered the White House in 1901, the idea of conservation had not yet found its way into the public mind," writes Jim Posewitz, author of *Rifle in Hand: How Wild America Was Saved*. "When he left office in 1909, he had implanted the idea of conservation into our culture and enriched our future prospects with 230 million acres of designated public forests, wildlife refuges, bird preserves, parks, national monuments, and game ranges."

Roosevelt's mentor, the naturalist and hunter George Bird Grinnel, had traveled through the West when the great herds of elk and pronghorn and bison still flowed over the Plains. Grinnell founded the prototypical sporting magazine *Forest and Stream* (later *Field & Stream*), and argued for the preservation of the wildlife and wild country that was left. He later founded the first Audubon Society and was instrumental in creating Glacier and Yellowstone national parks.

Together, Roosevelt, Grinnell and nine others founded the Boone and Crockett Club, which called for an end to market hunting, the protection of American bison and the establishment of game laws—radical changes in the way Americans viewed wildlife. (The Boone and Crockett Club is still around; it owns a sprawling ranch on Montana's Rocky Mountain Front dedicated to wildlife habitat, research and education. The Conservancy holds a conservation easement on the property.)

Important Conservation Laws

The low point for North American wildlife is considered to be 1910. By the 1930s, "[t]here was still not much game to hunt anywhere, but there was a lot of hope among American hunters," writes Posewitz. In that decade, hunters and gun companies sponsored two laws that have funded the most far-reaching restoration of wildlife and habitat in history.

The Federal Aid in Wildlife Restoration Act, popularly known as the Pittman-Robertson Act, created an 11 percent tax on sporting firearms and ammunition and a 10 percent tax on handguns to support wildlife conservation and to promote hunter safety. In the 75 years since it was enacted, Pittman-Robertson has raised more than $5 billion for conservation. Those funds will contribute more than $233 million this year [2006], mainly to support wildlife management areas that provide habitat and public access for everything from hiking and fishing to bird-watching and hunting.

The other law, the Migratory Bird Hunting and Conservation Stamp Act, requires waterfowl hunters aged 16 and older to possess a valid federal hunting stamp, commonly known as a duck stamp. Sales of the stamps have brought in nearly $700 million since the program's inception in 1934 and have helped to purchase and establish 5.2 million acres of the National Wildlife Refuge system. During the 2002–2003 hunting season, duck-stamp sales brought in almost $28 million, and 98 cents of every dollar went to purchase habitat for waterfowl—habitat that also serves every other creature that walks, swims, crawls or flies there. The U.S. Fish and Wildlife Service estimates that one-third of the nation's threatened and endangered species live on one or more of the refuges.

Opening Doors

According to the National Shooting Sports Foundation, between the Pittman-Robertson Act, the sale of duck stamps, and the sale of state game and fish licenses, hunters and anglers currently contribute about $4.7 million a day to wildlife conservation and protection. But in addition to spending power, what the sporting community has in abundance is political clout.

"The people that buy hunting and fishing licenses in this country have one thing in common: They vote," says Dave Nomsen, vice president of Pheasants Forever, which has worked closely with the Conservancy on wetlands and prairie conservation projects.

"In the past few years, we've had unprecedented access to the [George W. Bush] administration in Washington. We've been very vocal about our concerns, especially in protecting the funding for programs like Conservation Reserve and Wetlands Reserve." (Pheasants Forever, the Conservancy and 20

Hunters Aid in Species Preservation

Although some may find the fact surprising, outdoor sportsmen proposed and carried out virtually all of the initiatives that saved important U.S. game species from extinction. Indeed, most funding for the research into wildlife needs and habitat preservation still is provided by hunters. If Africa's diverse wildlife is to survive, it too likely will owe that survival to hunters.

H. Sterling Burnett,
"Hunters: Founders and Leaders of Wildlife Conservation,"
Brief Analysis from National Center for Policy Analysis,
November 12, 2001.

other sporting and conservation organizations worked this year to urge Congress to restore funding to the Wetlands Reserve Program.) Nomsen adds, "I think we are looking at a day where that door will always be open to the fishing and hunting groups, no matter [which party is] in the White House."

Nomsen attributes that open door to the formation of large umbrella groups like the Theodore Roosevelt Conservation Partnership (TRCP) and American Wildlife Conservation Partners that unite dozens of sportsmen's groups under one banner. "TRCP is doing a lot of new things," he says, "like engaging union members, who may not belong to any conservation organizations now, but they are sportsmen, and they share a lot of our common concerns."

Both Sides Benefit

From the sporting groups' perspective, the Conservancy opens a lot of doors as well. "The Conservancy has great green credentials," says Steve Moyer, a vice president at Trout Unlimited. Furthermore, smaller organizations like Trout (with approximately 150,000 members) can't begin to tap into the kinds of money the Conservancy brings to projects. Moyer notes, for example, that in a joint $50 million effort to remove dams from Maine's Penobscot River—an important spawning and nursery ground for endangered Atlantic salmon—Trout Unlimited is largely relying on the Conservancy's expertise in raising money from state and federal agencies.

For Keith Lenard—who worked for the Conservancy before going to the Elk Foundation—the two groups started in different parts of the conservation world, and traveled paths that inevitably converged. "I look at the creation of the Conservancy in the 1950s, when hunters were still the driving force of conservation—really the only force," he says. "Then land trusts like the Conservancy created a whole new model, and started to lead the hunters along to where we are now."

The potential of the convergence, Lenard believes, is only beginning to be realized. "The hook-and-bullet crowd . . . [is] still not a mainstream conservation movement. But we bring a whole new group of people into the room with the same goals. There's a whole lot of cross-pollination going on now."

Projects Large and Small

Nationwide, the Conservancy has worked with sporting groups to advocate for policies that favor conservation, to raise public funds for conservation, to restore rivers, to preserve working forests and to maintain public access to industrial forests that otherwise would have been sold to private developers.

The Conservancy has worked with hunting and fishing organizations on projects large and small. In South Carolina, the Conservancy is working with the 600,000-member Ducks Unlimited to protect large parts of the 1.6-million acre ACE Basin—the coastal region where the Ashepoo, Combahee and Edisto rivers converge. More than 160,000 acres have been protected so far. Meanwhile, in Clinton County, Pennsylvania, the Conservancy works with the 20-member West Branch

Hunt Club, which is aiding the restoration efforts of forest ecologists by helping to control the white-tailed deer population.

In one especially complex partnership, the Conservancy joined forces in 2003 with the Conservation Fund, the Elk Foundation and the Wild Turkey Federation in Tennessee to protect more than 75,000 acres and prevent the fragmentation of huge blocks of forest. Together, they and other groups helped unite a patchwork of state wildlife management areas with forestlands in Tennessee's Cumberland Mountains. The forestlands were being sold by coal and timber companies and would surely have been developed.

The deal drew public support largely because the groups' work ensured that hunting and fishing would be allowed to continue.

"That connection to hunting and fishing groups is where we're headed in Tennessee," says Scott Davis, who directs the Conservancy's work in the state. "The Tennessee Wildlife Resources Agency knows that it's not about a single species. What's good for a golden-winged warbler is good for a wild turkey. What's good for a freshwater mussel is good for a smallmouth bass. . . . It's about an intact forest and clean water, which is good for everybody."

For Bruce Kidman, director of government relations for the Conservancy in Maine, maintaining public access for hunting is critical to the organization's work: "Public access, on the face of it, has very little to do with the mission of the Conservancy. . . . But if you are going to live in a community, you have to find the common ground, and in Maine, that is access for hunting and fishing."

Hunting helps foster a relationship to the land that is crucial to future conservation efforts, adds Brian van Eerden, who manages more than 15,000 acres of Conservancy lands in southeastern Virginia, almost all of it leased to hunting clubs.

"Aldo Leopold [an environmentalist and hunter and fisherman] told us that everything is connected to everything else in nature," says van Eerden, "and we can see how sportsmen share this idea on such an intimate level with their children, passing these powerful experiences on from generation to generation. As we become more urbanized, we see things as more compartmentalized, and ecosystems do not function that way."

Stakes Are High

To be sure, there will always be issues on which some conservationists and hunters disagree—such as the protection of big carnivores and regulations such as the Endangered Species Act.

But it's possible to bridge the divide, says Gary Kania, who until recently was the Conservancy's liaison with the U.S. Fish and Wildlife Service and now works with the Congressional Sportsmen's Foundation. "There are enough goals that are the same," says Kania, who has also worked for the National Rifle Association [NRA]. "The NRA is not the Conservancy, but the NRA represents a lot of hunters, and what do hunters want, primarily? They want habitat for wildlife. We may disagree about other things, but we can argue about that later. First, we can use our common goals to leverage resources and get things done now."

Matt Miller of the Conservancy in Idaho says such partnerships are urgently needed: "I have been a hunter my whole life, growing up in Pennsylvania, and you see all the places that you've hunted and fished—the place that I ran my traplines when I was young—get swallowed up by sprawl. Sometime, even in high school, I realized that if we didn't do something, it would all be gone. It's why I became a conservationist in the first place."

The Sierra Club's Semcer knows there are differences in how environmentalists and hunters view the world, but says,

"I'd ask people on either side, 'Do we have the luxury of questioning people's motives who want to preserve the natural world?"

"We are at a point in history where the stakes are way high," says Semcer, "and if we don't trust each other, we all lose."

> "We are permitting the trophy hunting
> of the strongest, healthiest, and most
> powerful animals—those that should
> be leading their families and passing
> their genes on to future generations are
> being eradicated."

Hunting Contributes to Animal Species Extinction

Jane Goodall

In this viewpoint, Jane Goodall discusses the way in which hunting and other wildlife trade is driving species to extinction. Goodall notes that wildlife trade is destroying animal populations by reversing natural selection and calls for an international solution to the problem. Jane Goodall is an author, lecturer, conservationist, and the world's foremost authority on chimpanzees.

As you read, consider the following questions:

1. What is the only way that Goodall feels the trend of species extinction can be reversed?
2. What are some specific examples that Goodall offers of ways in which humans consume wildlife?

3. How have some countries addressed the issue of species extinction, according to Goodall?

In a world that seems to grow smaller with each passing year, human beings continue to consume with a voracious and insatiable appetite. We are consuming natural resources at an unprecedented rate and seem obsessed with "Band-Aid" solutions to environmental problems.

A Crisis in the Loss of Species

I have spent my life working with chimpanzees in Africa and am increasingly concerned about the fate of not just individual populations, but the species in general.

Talk is useful in addressing the problems, education is crucial, but until we unite and together develop and implement local and global solutions to the wildlife crisis, we will continue to lose species. It is time we recognized that our appetite is causing extinction.

Consumption of Wildlife

Wildlife trade is one of the greatest threats faced by animals around the world.

We are consuming wildlife for fashion, traditional medicine, souvenirs, trophy hunting, and bushmeat. We have commodified wildlife to the extent that an ideology has developed that wildlife can only remain if it "pays its way"—otherwise it is superfluous.

What are the long-term implications of such an ideology?

We are permitting the trophy hunting of the strongest, healthiest and most powerful animals—those that should be leading their families and passing their genes on to future generations are being eradicated.

Wildlife trade is destroying natural selection processes that have allowed species to evolve, thrive and survive. We need to consider that we are not only affecting individual species, but

Bushmeat Trade
Devastates the Environment

The latest global conservation crisis is the result of massive, unregulated hunting of mammals, birds, and reptiles for human consumption—the so-called bushmeat trade. Vast areas of virgin forest have been penetrated by logging roads and laid to waste by giant timber companies. Hunters travel these once inaccessible areas, snare or shoot everything from rodents to elephants, and transport the meat to market. The process began some 20 years ago in Asia, giving rise to a new conservation term: empty-forest syndrome. . . . [The] logging juggernaut is rolling through West and Central Africa's rain forests and through South and Central America. Burgeoning human populations, rising living standards, and conflict are also driving the demand for bushmeat. Annual consumption by 25 million people has reached more than 1 million metric tons in the Congo Basin alone— the equivalent of 4 million cattle.

Michael Satchell, "Hunting to Extinction:
A Wildlife Crisis is Forcing Conservationists to Rethink Their Tactics,"
U.S. News & World Report, *October 9, 2000, vol. 129, no. 14. p. 1.*

entire ecosystems and biodiversity. Intact ecosystems deliver the greatest benefits to communities—for both humans and animals.

We need to understand that international trade in wildlife does not solve poverty nor does it benefit conservation. International trade often drives dynamics that vacuum key species from ecosystems, leaving behind devastated habitats poor of life and livelihoods.

Very few parties benefit from the trade, and the cost is so great it is incalculable.

Working on Solutions

The Convention on International Trade in Endangered Species of Flora and Fauna meets in Thailand this month [October 2004].

Among the proposals on the table is a request by South Africa and Namibia to trade in ivory, elephant hair and leather for commercial purposes. This is despite opposition from many African nations who recognize that permitting any legal trade in elephant products, particularly in ivory, fuels the illegal market, which threatens global elephant populations.

Japan is proposing the downlisting of the certain stocks of minke whales in a move toward the resumption of commercial whaling.

However, there is some good news.

Kenya is rallying to prevent South Africa's and Namibia's proposals and to pave the way for lasting solutions for elephants and their habitats by requesting a 20-year moratorium for any ivory sale proposal and the closure of domestic markets.

Australia and Madagascar are proposing greater protection for the great white shark through the endangered species convention, and the United States and Indonesia are working toward increased protection for a number of Asian freshwater turtle species.

Also at the endangered species convention, the European Union is calling for the world to unite to solve the bushmeat crisis. While these are positive steps, it cannot be denied that there is a shift in the convention to support "sustainable" trade. This is why it is so important that nongovernmental organizations, such as the International Fund for Animal Welfare, continue to work tirelessly to ensure the real purpose of the convention is not forgotten—that is, conservation. Climate change, environmental devastation and the global trade in wildlife are all taking their toll.

We must continue to work for today, through conventions such as the one on endangered species but also for tomorrow through our young people.

By educating young people around the world, we can build respect for life and an appreciation of animals for what they are, not what use they are to us. We must build an appetite for conservation, not consumption. If we encourage young people throughout the world to learn about the problems we face, together we will find the solutions we need. And we can create a world that is big enough for us all.

> "However much some may blanch at the thought, that combination of a steady income plus minimal impact can make well-managed trophy hunting one of the best tools in the conservationists' toolbox."

Hunting Provides an Economic Motive for Maintaining Wildlife Habitats

Bob Holmes

In this viewpoint, Bob Holmes discusses the conservationists' use of large fees paid by trophy hunters to save endangered animals. He notes that although there are possible risks to the trophy animals' gene pool, social structure, and population numbers, the trickle-down hunting revenue may be the best answer to boost conservation's low funds. Bob Holmes is a writer for New Scientist *magazine.*

As you read, consider the following questions:

1. According to Holmes, what are the three parts needed for an effective conservation effort?

Bob Holmes, "Bag A Trophy, Save A Species," *New Scientist*, January 6, 2007, pp. 6–7. Copyright © 2007 Reed Business Information, UK, a division of Reed Elsevier Inc. Reproduced by permission.

2. What impact does Holmes say that trophy hunting could have on the social hierarchies of the target animal populations?

3. What effect can occur when trophy hunting is done just outside protected wildlife areas, according to Holmes?

Imagine conservation as a three-legged stool. You need the wildlife, you need local people to be committed to conservation ... and you need people to hunt down rare animals and kill them.

"When one of those legs isn't there, the whole thing falls apart," says Joe Hosmer, vice-president of Safari Club International, a hunting advocacy group based in Tucson, Arizona. Yes, the way to save wild animals, hunting advocates say, is to hunt them—or more precisely, to extract astronomical sums from rich hunters for the privilege of shooting a few prize specimens.

The Economics of Trophy Hunting

Perhaps more surprisingly, many conservation biologists see hunting in a similar light. Hunting can be a positive force, they say, because it provides an economic motive for maintaining wildlife habitats. "Without hunting many of these areas would be converted to cattle pasture, and there would be a rapid loss of wildlife," says Peter Lindsey, a conservation biologist at the University of Zimbabwe in Harare and author of a survey of trophy hunting in Africa. When it works, the jobs and money generated by hunting also give local residents an incentive to suppress poaching and keep animals live and on the hoof rather than in their cooking pot.

A few countries outside Africa, notably Pakistan, have successfully married hunting with conservation. However, in many parts of the world, trophy hunting has fallen far short of its potential for conservation. Even apparently sustainable hunting quotas may carry subtle dangers for target species, and some argue that the supposed benefits are overstated.

"Generally speaking trophy hunting takes place on marginal land not suitable for agriculture," says Will Travers of the Born Free Foundation, a conservation group based in the UK. "The best agricultural land is already used for agriculture." Trophy hunting is a growing industry in southern and eastern Africa, with hunters willing to pay tens of thousands of dollars for a safari that might bag them an elephant or a Cape buffalo. In Asia, too, some hunters will pay up to $30,000 to hunt scarce mountain sheep such as the argali, and a few prized trophies such as bighorn sheep in Alberta, Canada, have attracted as much as a million dollars in fees.

"The underlying theme is the enormous amount of money that people are willing to spend. That can be an enormous force for conservation," says Marco Festa-Bianchet, a wildlife biologist at the University of Sherbrooke, Quebec, in Canada.

Photo-tourism—the other main way of deriving income from wildlife—can also generate large amounts of money. Kenya, which does not allow trophy hunting, estimates that tourism generated $840 million in 2006, says Travers. However, hunters are often willing to travel to less scenic or politically unstable regions, providing an irreplaceable source of income. Even where the eventual goal is to generate income from tourism, hunting can help ease—and finance—the transition from degraded cattle pastures to a thriving natural ecosystem, says Lindsey.

Industry Self-Regulation

Most conservation biologists don't think that trophy hunters will shoot enough animals to push their prey to extinction. The hunters take almost exclusively males, so—in theory, at least—the birth rate should be unaffected as long as enough males remain to fertilise all the females. To charge their clients top dollar, hunting operators need to provide a good chance

Financial Contributions of Hunters

Whether members of a national organization or a local club, organized sporting enthusiasts are often the ones who put practical conservation to work in the individual wood lot, field or stream. It is estimated that hunters spend more than $690 million a year developing wildlife habitat through licenses, tags, permits and other fees to hunt on private land. Local clubs and their members work with the owners of large tracts of private land to open more acreage for a wide range of outdoor recreational uses. They consistently urge their fellow outdoor enthusiasts to respect the property of others and to observe the rules of outdoor etiquette.

The National Shooting Sports Foundation Inc.,
The Hunter and Conservation, *2006.*

of bagging a trophy-quality animal. A greedy operator who takes too many animals will soon have a hard time drawing clients to a depleted area, says Lindsey.

But that smooth self-regulation only applies where hunting operators are tied to a particular area, as they are in many parts of Africa. Where that local tie is missing, as it is in much of Asia, operators can simply shift away from depleted areas, so they have little incentive to tread lightly. "Inevitably, it is run as a business. At some point the benefits to the businessman don't necessarily coincide with the benefits to conservation. The reality is if you can make more money by wiping out the resource quickly, that's what you do," says Festa-Bianchet. Travers agrees. "Hunting licences are offered on relatively short time frames of three to four years, so this can be seen as a short-term gain opportunity."

Nor are hunters likely to take the conservation initiative in such cases. "We will support any legal form of hunting," says

Hosmer. "If our government and the foreign government legally will allow us to hunt a species, then we will support that."

Often, too, very few of the dollars generated by hunting end up in conservationists' hands. "If you're supposed to be getting enough money to do some conservation, it's just not there," says Rich Harris, a wildlife biologist affiliated with the University of Montana in Missoula who has served as a consultant for some Chinese trophy-hunting programmes.

Drawbacks

Even where hunting is managed smoothly, and when hunting revenue does trickle down to conservation projects, it may cause subtle genetic damage to wildlife populations. The large antlers, horns or tusks that make trophy animals so attractive to hunters evolved as signals to help females pick mates with the best genes. Trophy hunters remove these good genes every time they bag an animal. In bighorn sheep in Alberta, Canada, hunting pressure has led to smaller-horned sheep of lower genetic quality, Festa-Bianchet and his colleagues reported three years ago. Similar pressures may account for an increasing number of tuskless elephants in Africa and Asia.

There are other easily overlooked potential knock-on effects. By removing dominant males, for example, hunters may increase the rate of turnover in social hierarchies. This can be a serious problem in species such as lions, where males that take over a pride typically kill all the cubs sired by the previous male. Every time the head of a pride is killed by hunters, all the cubs may be lost also, says Andrew Loveridge, a wildlife biologist at the University of Oxford.

Lions also illustrate what Loveridge calls the "vacuum effect", in which hunting just outside a protected area can siphon animals away from the park. Heavy hunting pressure in safari areas just outside Hwange National Park in Zimbabwe, for example, led to the loss of 72 per cent of tagged adult male lions to hunters over a five-year period, Loveridge found in a study published [in January 2007]. Most of these males were replaced by lions from the park, diminishing the numbers within it.

Occasionally this vacuum effect may run in reverse, to the benefit of wildlife. In Alberta, for example, some bighorn rams shelter in the safety of Banff and Jasper national parks during the hunting season and then roam outside the parks to breed. This returns good genes to the population outside the park and helps reverse the genetic erosion caused by trophy hunting, says Festa-Bianchet.

Biologists have little idea how serious these subtler genetic and population impacts of hunting will prove to be. "We just haven't thought much about this. Maybe it's a major concern, maybe it's nothing to worry about," says Festa-Bianchet. Still, wildlife managers may well want to move more cautiously in light of the risk. In Zimbabwe, for example, quotas for lion hunting have been cut back by 50 per cent in the past two years to prevent overhunting.

The Bottom Line

The flow of money may be unaffected, though. "The price of lion hunting has gone through the roof," says Lindsey, "which is excellent for conservationists because we want to see the fewest animals removed for the highest price."

However much some may blanch at the thought, that combination of a steady income plus minimal impact can make well-managed trophy hunting one of the best tools in the conservationists' toolbox.

> *"Hunting, then, is not a utility for thinning out deer herds but more of a liability to their health and longevity."*

Hunting Destroys the Natural Population Ratio of the Hunted Animal

Jeremy Alcorn

In this viewpoint, Jeremy Alcorn refutes arguments that hunting is an effective method of animal population control. Alcorn reviews the negative effects hunting has on animal population, focusing on the disruption of natural selection. Jeremy Alcorn is an animal rights activist and author of the Web site VeganVanguard.com.

As you read, consider the following questions:

1. What variables control the number of animals in a deer herd, according to Alcorn?

2. What does Alcorn say is the effect on the population of a deer herd of an increase in the number of females?

Jeremy Alcorn, "Hunting as a Method of Population Control," *www.veganvanguard.com*, 2005. Reproduced by permission of the author.

3. According to Alcorn, what negative effect could hunting have on deer populations over the long term?

Among the variety of reasons provided for the continuation of hunting we find an appeal from the standpoint of conservation presented in the form of population control. While there is information regarding the effectiveness of hunting towards the goal of population control, there is also research that would suggest otherwise. This information lends a degree of plausibility to the notion that population control methods such as hunting constitute more of a risk than initially thought.

Deer herd populations are controlled by a number of variables. For the purposes of this article we shall be examining the effects of population numbers based on the availability of food and the male-to-female ratio. Briefly examined is the severity of winter casualties.

Winter Attrition

The first variable we should explore is one that we will return to a number of times in the course of this article. In climates that experience winters where vegetation is adversely affected, deer herd populations drop because of a process referred to as "die-off". Winter die-off is where the old and/or weak segments of a population succumb to elements such as cold and starvation. Winter die-off helps to alleviate food shortages for the surviving members of a population and has the effect of eliminating weaker genetic lines. By eliminating some members of a population whose genetic code causes them to be among the least adaptable, future members will be better able to survive. This is what is referred to as natural selection and it ensures that the future population will be equipped with the traits that are best suited for survival.

Food Availability

Food, and its availability, is another factor that relates to the number of deaths as well as births. Predictably, a lack of food can cause deaths from starvation, but another factor may be far more important in controlling populations.

When food is scarce the birth rate of a population will decrease. This is due to biological changes brought about by malnutrition. Malnutrition causes male deer to become less virile than what is present during nutritionally adequate years. As for the obverse gender, female deer when undernourished will encounter reduced or, in extreme situations, complete cessation of ovulation (this is in keeping with studies of malnourished humans as well). Both of these occurrences limit the number of births and help to keep the population in balance with the availability of food.

Male-to-Female Ratios

Now let's briefly address the dynamics behind the male-to-female ratios amongst deer populations. The natural outcome of deer births rest around fifty-percent male and fifty-percent female, that is, an equal number (1:1) of males and females are born each year. The birth ratio when it varies usually favors more male births than females. However, this difference is usually not significant.

Birth ratios are important because during mating season a single male deer will mate with as many females as are receptive to him. If there were more females than males, the birth rate would increase each year. This is especially important considering that some females, depending on the quantity and quality of food, will give birth to more than one fawn. A given area of land can only provide food for a limited number of deer. So it is advantageous that half of a population be male, because more females will lead to more births and, subsequently, less food.

Hunting Disrupts Victims' Social Structure

The influence of hunting is as follows. Firstly, a large percentage of members of the wild boar society is killed every year. This is compensated for by feeding throughout the year and especially during winter. Often, primary targets for trophy hunters are the lonely males, and if not available, then the older and bigger females. The only protected ones are the females with young.

As a consequence, no wild boar is older than 6 years anymore! Most are between one and two years old! That means the structure of the society is totally destroyed. What remains is a group of youngsters, disoriented and unable to survive independently, so that they become totally dependent on feeding by humans. They have not been given the chance to learn anything from their elders, because they are dead. And they have not [had] the chance to get enough experience to forward to [the] next generation, because they will likely die before they have matured.

Martin Balluch, "Thoughts on Hunting and Fishing,"
Animal Concerns. *www.articles.animalconcerns.org*
/ar-voices/archive/hunt_thoughts.html.

The Negative Effects of Hunting

The natural 50/50 birth ratio is often offset by the actions of hunters, either intentionally or accidentally. As we will see below, some believe the ratio of female to male deer in the wild is 8:1 respectively. Hunters who participate in big game hunting involve themselves in the search for a trophy. I know hunters who continually seek to "bag", or kill, a big buck; often they succeed. In the case of deer hunting, a trophy is a male deer with a larger number of antler points or tines (which branch off of the animal's main antler beams) than what is normally seen.

Because many hunters would like to kill large bucks, states try to limit this by issuing certain types of permits. These permits are "either-sex", which allows a hunter to choose which sex deer to kill, or "antlerless", meaning a hunter can only kill a deer with no antlers or antlers coming in under a specified height. Many hunters possessing an either-sex permit set out to kill primarily male deer. In fact, local research has determined that of the either-sex permits issued, 87% of those were used for male deer. To overcome this, states issue antlerless permits to some applicants. However, even with these permits in hand, hunters sometimes kill male deer because they were too young to have developed antlers, and were resultantly mistaken for females. Again, local research indicates that of the antlerless permits issued, 29% of those are used for male deer rather than females. This is perfectly legal, but it can further skew the population ratio. Also, not all antlerless permits are filled every year, leaving to chance the situation of too few female deer being killed. Given the hunter's desire to kill a trophy buck, the killing of young bucks when attempting to kill females, and the plausibility that female deer will be underkilled each year; it is easy to concede that the population can be thrown off balance. In Illinois, for instance, the state's leading employed biologist Dr. Paul Shelton stated, "During the 1999 season we didn't take as many does as we should have." This statement indicates that indeed, at times female deer are not killed in the numbers needed.

Implications of Skewed Sex Ratio

When more female deer survive than do males, the subsequent year(s) will produce more fawns in the spring. Add to this factor the decrease in food usage caused by hunting season deaths, winter die-off, and nonhuman predation, and a population increase will inevitably follow. Peter Muller, board member of Wildlife Watch, Inc bases his example on an 80:20 sex ratio (80 female: 20 males). With such a ratio present

Muller contends that,

> Nature's mechanisms that adjust the population to the
> browse will now miscalculate and cause an overpopulation.
> Based on 50-50 ratio, a herd of 400 will produce a maxi-
> mum 50-animal net gain assuming a 100 animal winter die-
> off and 150-fawn increase from the remaining 150 does.
> Based on an 80-20 ratio, a 400 animal herd will produce a
> 140 animal increase, assuming again a 100 animal winter
> die-off, but this time 240 does will give birth to 240 fawns
> instead of 150 does giving birth to 150 fawns. With the ratio
> distorted at 80-20, the population will increase to 540 in-
> stead of 450.

Two things can happen as a result of this. The first is that a
die-off greater than normal may result either from starvation
or disease. The second, and far worse, scenario is that the increased herd population survives only to further inflate its
population for the upcoming mating season.

From the Field

Certain historical accounts lend credence to the second scenario stated above. Consider Missouri's conservation efforts at
increasing deer populations. Around the turn of the 20th century Missouri's deer population consisted of "395 deer in 23
counties" [according to the Missouri Department of Conser-
vation]. Missouri was in danger of losing one of its species.
Because the populations were severely below natural levels,
Missouri soon banned hunting (unregulated hunting was a
reason for the decline). In 1944, Missouri implemented a
"bucks only" hunting season in an effort to increase the herd's
population. This allows more births in the spring than if the
females were killed. Due in part to this special hunting season,
Missouri now is experiencing a population of around 750,000
deer.

Hunting is no doubt central in affecting population, but
with an increasing body of research it is seen by many as a

dangerous gamble. It is true that the immediate problem of population control is resolved. For instance, the Missouri Department of Conservation estimates that 200,000 deer are killed annually by some 400,000 hunters. While this seems as if hunting has served a vital purpose in reducing herd numbers, some believe that the stage is set for a population increase. It seems as if the second scenario is sound given that deer herd populations almost everywhere are increasing.

By the preceding account, if hunting controls population at all, it serves to elevate population levels to the eventual point of starvation on a wider scale than what occurs naturally. Given the natural propensity for deer herds to biologically control their population numbers, the strain humans place on those reproductive tendencies serves to exacerbate the dynamics of herd demographics while increasing population numbers simultaneously. Until society comes to realize the folly of its conservation efforts (i.e. hunting), the unnatural trend towards increasing population numbers will likely become more of a problem than it is today. Hunting, then, is not a utility for thinning out deer herds but more of a liability to their health and longevity.

Periodical Bibliography

*The following articles have been selected to supplement
the diverse views presented in this chapter.*

Ron Baker   "How Hunting Contributes to Species Extinction," undated. www.articles.animalconcerns.org.

Natalie Bouaravong   "A Human Taste for Rarity Spells Disaster for Endangered Species," *EurekAlert*, November 27, 2006. www.eurekalert.org/pub_releases/2006-11/plos-aht112106.php.

Tom Chesshyre   "The Conservation Conundrum," *Geographical*, September 2005.

Gerhard R Damm   "Hunters and Conservationists Are Natural Partners!," *African Indaba eNewsletter*, September 2006. www.biggame.org/News/African IndabaVol4.pdf.

Claudia Dreifus   "A Conversation with: Elizabeth Bennett; A Global Advocate for the Meal That Cannot Speak for Itself," *New York Times*, June 6, 2006.

Sid Evans   Heroes of Conservation. *Field & Stream (West ed.)*, October 2006.

Whitefield Gibbons   "Declining Hunter Still Good for the Environment," *Ecoviews*, November 13, 2005. www.uga.edu/srel.

The League Against Cruel Sports   "The Myth of Trophy Hunting as Conservation," December 2004. www.league.org.uk.

Peter Muller   "Hunting by Humans Perverse, Too Efficient— Nature Has Solutions," Committee to Abolish Sport Hunting, undated. www.all-creatures.org.

National Rifle Association   "Dollars: From Hunters, for Wildlife," National Rifle Association Headquarters, undated. www.nrahq.org/hunting/hunterdollars.asp.

CHAPTER 4

Is Hunting a Form of Cruelty to Animals?

Chapter Preface

On October 25, 2005, the *Washington Post* reported that an eight-year-old girl was credited with shooting the first bear of the Maryland bear-hunting season. After shooting the bear, the girl is quoted as saying that she was "really, really, really happy." The report of the young hunter sparked debate between hunters and animal rights activists. The Humane Society of the United States, a group whose stated purpose is to promote the protection of all animals and prevent animal cruelty, responded with concerns that young children and young bears were being unnecessarily exposed to the cruelty of hunting. The group also raised its standard concern that hunting violates animal rights. Hunters interviewed in the same *Washington Post* article, however, expressed excitement at seeing children out hunting after concerns had been raised in recent years over the decreasing numbers of hunters. Hunting proponents viewed the presence of the eight-year-old as a hopeful sign. These interviewees did not display any concerns about a young girl out hunting or about her violating animal rights. The opposing positions that arose over the news of the young hunter are representative of the debate over the rights of animals and the practice of hunting.

The struggle over animal rights has been debated in increasingly diverse forums since hunting for food and protection transitioned into hunting as a sport in the twentieth century. Many animal rights activists feel that animals should have the same rights as humans, including the rights to not be harassed, stressed, stalked, and killed by hunters. However, even the positions of individual members and organizations within the animal rights movement vary.

Some groups, such as the Humane Society of the United States, recognize that certain people still need to hunt animals for food and survival and so support this form of hunting.

Other organizations, such as Friends of Animals, believe that animals should not be hunted for food or sport. As a counterpoint, most hunters view hunting as a natural outdoor pastime that cements the bond between humans and nature while humanely and respectfully pitting man against animal. When asked about the rights of animals, hunters also have a range of opinions, but the majority view is that human rights override animal rights. The opposing sides in the hunting debate often voice their opinions in the political arena as government officials introduce legislation regulating or deregulating various aspects of hunting. The disagreement over hunting and whether or not it is a form of animal cruelty is heated and personal. The authors of the viewpoints in this chapter expand upon the positions of hunters and animal rights advocates as they debate whether or not hunting constitutes cruelty to animals.

> "Although it was a crucial part of humans' survival 100,000 years ago, hunting is now nothing more than a violent form of recreation."

Sport Hunting Is an Unnecessary Form of Cruelty to Animals

People for the Ethical Treatment of Animals

In this viewpoint, the organization People for the Ethical Treatment of Animals (PETA) presents its opinion that hunting is unnecessary and cruel to animals. PETA states that hunting causes animals pain, suffering, and stress as part of a sport that uses conservation as a shield. The authors offer humane alternatives to hunting for population control of animals. People for the Ethical Treatment of Animals is an animal rights organization that believes that animals have rights and deserve to have their best interests taken into consideration, regardless of whether they are useful to humans.

As you read, consider the following questions:

1. On what public lands is hunting allowed, according to PETA?

2. How often are hunters unable to retrieve fatally wounded animals, according to PETA?

3. What does this viewpoint describe as some humane alternatives to hunting?

Although it was a crucial part of humans' survival 100,000 years ago, hunting is now nothing more than a violent form of recreation that the vast majority of hunters does not need for subsistence. Hunting has contributed to the extinction of animal species all over the world, including the Tasmanian tiger and the great auk.

Less than 5 percent of the U.S. population hunts, yet hunting is permitted in many wildlife refuges, national forests, state parks, and on other public lands. Forty percent of hunters slaughter and maim millions of animals on public land every year, and by some estimates, poachers kill just as many animals illegally.

Pain and Suffering

Many animals suffer prolonged, painful deaths when they are injured but not killed by hunters. A member of the Maine Bowhunters Alliance estimates that 50 percent of animals who are shot with crossbows are wounded but not killed. A study of 80 radio-collared white-tailed deer found that of the 22 deer who had been shot with "traditional archery equipment," 11 were wounded but not recovered by hunters. Twenty percent of foxes who have been wounded by hunters are shot again; 10 percent manage to escape, but "starvation is a likely fate" for them, according to one veterinarian. A South Dakota Department of Game, Fish, and Parks biologist estimates that more than 3 million wounded ducks go "unretrieved" every year. A British study of deer hunting found that 11 percent of deer who'd been killed by hunters died only after being shot two or more times and that some wounded deer suffered for more than 15 minutes before dying.

Hunting disrupts migration and hibernation patterns and destroys families. For animals like wolves, who mate for life and live in close-knit family units, hunting can devastate entire communities. The stress that hunted animals suffer—caused by fear and the inescapable loud noises and other commotion that hunters create—also severely compromises their normal eating habits, making it hard for them to store the fat and energy that they need in order to survive the winter.

Blood-Thirsty and Profit-Driven

To attract more hunters (and their money), federal and state agencies implement programs—often called "wildlife management" or "conservation" programs—that are designed to boost the number of "game" species. These programs help to ensure that there are plenty of animals for hunters to kill and, consequently, plenty of revenue from the sale of hunting licenses.

Duck hunters in Louisiana persuaded the state wildlife agency to direct $100,000 a year toward "reduced predator impact," which involved trapping foxes and raccoons so that more duck eggs would hatch, giving hunters more birds to kill. The Ohio Division of Wildlife teamed up with a hunter-organized society to push for clear-cutting (i.e., decimating large tracts of trees) in Wayne National Forest in order to "produce habitat needed by ruffed grouse."

In Alaska, the Department of Fish and Game is trying to increase the number of moose for hunters by "controlling" the wolf and bear populations. Grizzlies and black bears have been moved hundreds of miles away from their homes; two were shot by hunters within two weeks of their relocation, and others have simply returned to their homes. Wolves have been slaughtered in order to "let the moose population rebound and provide a higher harvest for local hunters." In the early 1990s, a program designed to reduce the wolf popula-

The Truth About Hunting

We must shoot deer, they tell us in Connecticut, to save the Audubon habitat. We must shoot wolves, we hear, to feed McGrath [Alaska]. Never mind that nonviolent strategies can rescue Audubon from its peril, or that aircraft can more easily airlift tofu burgers to famished McGrathans than hunt down wolves. The decision-makers aren't interested in nonhunting alternatives, whatever they may be—not because they may be cumbersome or cost a few dollars but because they would force on the decision-makers' consciousness a profoundly inconvenient truth about deer and wolves. Were the decision-makers to acknowledge that these sentient animals can experience pain, pleasure, suffering and enjoyment, they would find it impossible to defend a decision to shoot them.

William Mannetti,
"Shouting the Inconvenient Truth About Hunting,"
Friends of Animals, Spring 2004.
www.friendsofanimals.org/actionline.

tion backfired when snares failed to kill victims quickly and photos of suffering wolves were seen by an outraged public.

Nature Takes Care of Its Own

The delicate balance of ecosystems ensures their own survival—if they are left unaltered. Natural predators help maintain this balance by killing only the sickest and weakest individuals. Hunters, however, kill any animal whom they would like to hang over the fireplace—including large, healthy animals who are needed to keep the population strong. Elephant poaching is believed to have increased the number of tuskless animals in Africa, and in Canada, hunting has caused bighorn sheep's horn size to fall by 25 percent in the last 40 years; *Nature* magazine reports that "the effect on the populations' genetics is probably deeper."

Even when unusual natural occurrences cause overpopulation, natural processes work to stabilize the group. Starvation and disease can be tragic, but they are nature's ways of ensuring that healthy, strong animals survive and maintain the strength level of the rest of their herd or group. Shooting an animal because he or she *might* starve or become sick is arbitrary and destructive.

"Sport" hunting not only jeopardizes nature's balance, it also exacerbates other problems. For example, the transfer of captive-bred deer and elk between states for the purpose of hunting is believed to have contributed to the epidemic spread of chronic wasting disease (CWD). As a result, the U.S. Department of Agriculture (USDA) has given state wildlife agencies millions of dollars to "manage" deer and elk populations. The fatal neurological illness that affects these animals has been likened to mad cow disease, and while the USDA and the Centers for Disease Control and Prevention [CDC] claim that CWD has no relationship to any similar diseases that affect humans or farmed animals, the slaughter of deer and elk continues.

Another problem with hunting involves the introduction of exotic "game" animals who, if they're able to escape and thrive, pose a threat to native wildlife and established ecosystems. After a group of nonnative wild boars escaped from a private ranch and moved into the forests of Cambria County, Pa., the state of Pennsylvania drafted a bill prohibiting the importation of all exotic species of animals.

Canned Cruelty

Most hunting occurs on private land, where laws that protect wildlife are often inapplicable or difficult to enforce. On private lands that are set up as for-profit hunting reserves or game ranches, hunters can pay to kill native and exotic species in "canned hunts." These animals may be native to the area, raised elsewhere and brought in, or purchased from individuals who are trafficking in unwanted or surplus animals from zoos and circuses. They are hunted and killed for the sole purpose of providing hunters with a "trophy."

Canned hunts are becoming big business—there are an estimated 1,000 game preserves in the U.S. [Media mogul] Ted Turner, who owns more land than any other landowner in the country, operates 20 ranches, where hunters pay thousands of dollars to kill bison, deer, African antelopes, and turkeys.

Animals on canned-hunting ranches are often accustomed to humans and are usually unable to escape from the enclosures that they are confined to, which range in size from just a few yards to thousands of acres. Most of these ranches operate on a "no kill, no pay" policy, so it is in owners' best interests to ensure that clients get what they came for. Owners do this by offering guides who are familiar with animals' locations and habits, permitting the use of dogs, and supplying "feeding stations" that lure unsuspecting animals to food while hunters lie in wait.

Only a handful of states prohibit canned hunting, and there are no federal laws regulating the practice at this time. Congress is considering an amendment to the Captive Exotic Animal Protection Act that would prohibit the transfer, transportation, or possession of exotic animals "for entertainment or the collection of a trophy."

"Accidental" Victims

Hunting "accidents" destroy property and injure or kill horses, cows, dogs, cats, hikers, and other hunters. In 2006, Vice President Dick Cheney famously shot a friend while hunting quail on a canned-hunting preserve. According to the International Hunter Education Association, there are dozens of deaths and hundreds of injuries attributed to hunting in the United States every year—and that number only includes incidents involving humans. It is an ongoing problem, and one warden explained that "hunters seem unfamiliar with their firearms and do not have enough respect for the damage they can do."

A Humane Alternative

There are 30 million deer in the U.S., and because hunting has been an ineffective method to "control" populations (one Pennsylvania hunter "manages" the population and attracts deer by clearing his 600-acre plot of wooded land and planting corn), some wildlife agencies are considering other management techniques. Several recent studies suggest that sterilization is an effective, long-term solution to overpopulation. A method called TNR (trap, neuter, and return) has been tried on deer in Ithaca, N.Y., and an experimental birth-control vaccine is being used on female deer in Princeton, N.J. One Georgia study of 1,500 white-tailed deer on Cumberland Island concluded that "if females are captured, marked, and counted, sterilization reduces herd size, even at relatively low annual sterilization rates."

"No hunter wants to make an animal suffer needlessly, and it is not in the hunter's best interest to wound an animal that runs off, is panicked and difficult to locate for a second shot."

Sport Hunting Is Not Unnecessarily Cruel to Animals

Mike Lapierre

In this viewpoint, Mike Lapierre discusses hunting, its ethical implications, and the reasons it is not unnecessarily cruel to animals. Lapierre states that a hunter's goal is to humanely and accurately kill animals without causing them to suffer needlessly. He also discusses the natural defenses of game animals and hunters' role in conservation of wildlife habitat. Mike Lapierre is a hunter who runs the Back Country Journal hunting Web site.

As you read, consider the following questions:

1. What is the difference between a standard hunter and a poacher, according to Lapierre?

2. In Lapierre's view, how is a human hunter more humane than an animal predator?

Mike Lapierre, "On the Anti-Hunting Point of View," *www.backcountryjournal.com*, March 4, 2007. Reproduced by permission of the author.

3. What does Lapierre believe is the main underlying reason that animal predators have begun attacking pets and livestock?

If someone is uncomfortable with the idea of hunting, they shouldn't hunt and they shouldn't be pressured to hunt.

But to condemn hunting and hunters as being immoral or unethical and to insist it be stopped is highly problematic.

This really is a social issue about hatred, intolerance, prejudice and discrimination.

Hunting is no more or less moral and ethical than buying meat from a supermarket or raising one's own livestock for food.

In this day and age, we are detached from the realities of where our food comes from. It is acceptable to pay someone to kill the cows, pigs and chickens we purchase at the supermarket. It is also acceptable for a person to raise their own livestock for food. However, if I choose to hunt non-endangered animals during a legal hunting season, observing local laws, some will claim that I am no different from a violent criminal.

Hunters are not evil or maniacal. I have never met a hunter who "killed for the thrill" and left the carcass behind. I have never met a hunter who hunted endangered species or didn't observe local seasons and laws. This does happen from time to time and it is called poaching. Poaching is illegal and is very much frowned upon in the hunting community. To compare hunters to poachers is like comparing shoppers to shoplifters. To compare hunters to poachers is like saying that all men are rapists.

A Hunter's Goal Is to Be Humane

As far as whether or not hunting is humane, I can only say that a hunter is highly motivated to make an accurate, humane kill shot to the vital organs. This is both for the sake of the animal and for the sake of the hunter. No hunter wants to make an animal suffer needlessly, and it is not in the hunter's best interest to wound an animal that runs off, is panicked and difficult to locate for a second shot. When compared to cougars, wolves, alligators and other predators, the human hunter is perhaps the most humane hunter in the wild. Isn't it more humane to be shot from a distance unexpectedly than to be chased down and eaten alive?

Some people claim that game animals are defenseless and non-threatening. Cows, pigs and chickens are defenseless and non-threatening, but it is acceptable to pay someone to kill them so that we can eat them. Game animals on the other hand, can sometimes be very threatening. More importantly, game animals have very strong defenses. Their senses of smell and hearing are exponentially more sensitive than our own and these senses are used to aid in their survival.

Here is an example to illustrate this point: As humans, we are able to pick up a scent in the air from about 3 feet away. Dogs, about 30 feet. Whitetail Deer, 300 feet. A whitetail deer in the wild is an expert at using the wind strategically to survive and will run away the instant it smells or hears anything that is foreign. It is extremely difficult to sneak up on a game animal in the wild.

Hunting and Animal Predators

Some raise the point that hunters have killed off all of the natural predators and this is our self serving way of making hunting neccessary. This is a twisting of the facts. The facts are that as more and more wildlife habitat was developed for humans to live on, instances of predators attacking people, pets and livestock increased. This led to calls for liberal hunting seasons and bag limits on predators. That is why their numbers have been depleted. Did the hunters kill these predators? Yes. But the hunters were not the problem. In this instance, encroachment and development was and still is the problem. We are all to blame for this.

Fox Hunting Is Not Cruel

When we speak of suffering we may mean one or other of two things: first, physical pain; secondly, fear and stress. Fear and stress are a natural part of life in the wild, and the constant daily diet of all animals who live there. Pain usually comes through injury, and for a wild animal the normal result of injury is a slow and painful death. The hunted fox, if caught, is killed all but instantly—the number and weight of the hounds ensures that this is so. The fox's pain is less than the pain it would suffer from any other normal cause of death, since there is no possibility that a fox, once caught, should succumb to a lingering death through injury or trauma. Only the 'stress' of the chase could be considered as an addition to his sufferings—but this fear and stress are unavoidable parts of a process which compares favourably with any alternative. The average hunt lasts for 17 minutes, and more often than not ends in an escape. There is no attempt either to eke out the suffering of the fox or to deprive it of its natural defence, which is to fly from the danger. Seventeen minutes is, considered in context, arguably only a small portion of the fear experienced by a wild animal in the course of an ordinary day.

Roger Scrunton, "Fox-Hunting: The Modern Case," written submission to Lord Burns of the Committee of Inquiry into Hunting, 2000. www.huntinginquiry.gov.uk/evidence/scrunton.htm.

Hunters and Habitat Conservation

It is inaccurate to imply that hunters are unconcerned about depleting the resource. To the contrary. If we want our grandchildren's grandchildren to be able to hunt (and we do), we must be proactive about preserving and maintaining habitat for wildlife. Hunters are conservationists.

Every year millions of hunters' dollars pay for wildlife management. The Pittman-Robertson Act collects an 11% excise tax on firearms and ammunition and a 10% excise tax on handguns. These dollars are used to help government agencies purchase and maintain millions of forested acres known as Wildlife Management Areas (WMAs) which are enjoyed free of charge by hunters and non-hunters alike.

This important work is also done by volunteer organizations such as Ducks Unlimited, the National Wild Turkey Federation, Pheasants Forever and the Rocky Mountain Elk Foundation. Hunters spend a great deal of time and money to preserve, maintain and protect wildlife habitat. Hunters aren't the enemy of wildlife. Development is the enemy of wildlife.

Fear of the Unfamiliar

Some people are convinced that hunters are motivated to hunt because it gives them pleasure to watch an animal suffer and die. This could not be further from the truth. In fact, I would like to make a request of those who feel this way: *Please do not make assumptions about the motives of hunters.*

Many people who have never been exposed to hunting or who do not understand or agree with hunting make this assumption and this simply is not the way it is. If you are unsure about this, please ask questions of the hunters you know. Ask what hunting is to them. Ask what they get out of hunting and whether or not they hunt because it gives them pleasure to watch an animal suffer and die.

I have hunted all of my life and I grew up in a rural area where most of the people we knew hunted. I also work in the hunting industry as a booking agent for hunting trips. I speak with hundreds of hunters every year and I have spoken with and known thousands of hunters over the course of my life. Do I know everything there is to know about hunting? Absolutely not. But, in the course of interacting with all of these people, I have never once come across a person who hunts because it gives them pleasure to watch an animal suffer and die.

Why Hunters Hunt

What do we get out of hunting? What motivates otherwise sane and humane people to go out and kill other living things? Well, for me and for most of the hunters I have known it is for the challenge, the satisfaction and yes even the fun of doing something yourself.

It is the same challenge, satisfaction and fun that people get from gardening, from raising livestock for food, from doing their own home repairs, etc. For someone who has never been exposed to hunting or who does not understand or agree with hunting, this may be a difficult explanation to relate to, but it is true nonetheless.

Here is an example: When I was growing up, we raised chickens. Every fall, we would kill, pluck and prepare chickens for the freezer. Killing, plucking and preparing chickens wasn't the most pleasant work, but in the end, it was extremely satisfying (and delicious) to eat the chickens we had raised.

As children, this experience helped my brother and I to learn a great deal about the mysteries of life and death. It helped to make us that much more mindful and appreciative of where our food comes from and that a living being had to die in order for us to live.

For me, whether my food is bought from a store, raised by me or taken by me in the wild, it is all the same from an ethical perspective. I don't make an ethical distinction between killing a chicken that I have raised for food and going into the woods to hunt a game bird during a legal hunting season, observing local laws.

I must add that food I have either raised myself or taken in the wild is better tasting and more meaningful and satisfying than anything I could buy in a store. This is the challenge, the satisfaction and the fun that I am talking about.

Discrimination Against Hunters

One area of this debate that deeply troubles me is that this is a very serious diversity issue. How is comparing hunters to murderers and criminals different from racial/demographic profiling or stereotyping? This sort of thing is a prime example of hatred, intolerance, prejudice and discrimination.

It is unnacceptable to speak or act hatefully toward demographic groups based upon their race, religion, gender or sexual preference. But somehow it is ok to categorize responsible, law-abiding citizens who hunt and own firearms as violent criminals.

I'll give you an example: In many urban/suburban areas, fewer people have been exposed to guns and hunting than in rural areas. Consequently, it is much more difficult for some people to relate to gun owners and hunters. This makes gun owners and hunters easier for some people to condemn.

For instance, we have all heard about homosexuals in the workplace who are ostracized when their lifestyle is discovered. Some people have never known anyone who is a homosexual, so it is difficult for them to understand and relate to. Consequently, they make certain judgments and assumptions about that person's character and morals, and with a whisper campaign they go about destroying that person's reputation and do everything they can to make them look and feel like a freak.

Many gun owners and hunters experience this very same phenomenon. Thankfully, for homosexuals this is improving, but for hunters and gun owners it is getting worse by the minute.

All of this is wrong, of course. But sadly, it is human nature. For some reason, it is human instinct to condemn what we fear. We fear what we don't understand. We don't understand what we can't relate to.

How can we work to change this? How can we work to heal this? How can we work toward being more compassionate, understanding and tolerant of each other?

Condemning hunting and hunters, however well meaning, is a very serious social problem. It is exactly the same as condemning people of a different race, religion, gender or sexual preference.

When it comes to hunting, there are three categories of people:

- Hunters (people who hunt)

- Non-Hunters (people who do not hunt, but accept that other people hunt)

- Anti-Hunters (people who feel that hunting is immoral and unethical and condemn hunting and hunters)

What is hunting to you?

> *"The law should impose further regulation on hunting, scientific experiments, entertainment, and (above all) farming to ensure against unnecessary animal suffering."*

Animals Have Value and Are Not Human Resources to Be Hunted

Cass R. Sunstein

In the following viewpoint, Cass Sunstein discusses the reasons that the rights of animals exist and should be protected. He states that when the principles of animal rights are thoughtfully pondered, it is intuitive that they exist. Sunstein feels that state anticruelty laws should be expanded to protect animals from being hunted or used for unnecessary medical or scientific purposes. Cass Sunstein is an attorney and the Karl N. Llewellyn Distinguished Service Professor of Jurisprudence at the Law School and Department of Political Science of the University of Chicago.

Cass R. Sunstein, "The Rights of Animals," *The University of Chicago Law Review*, vol. 70, no. 1, Winter 2003, p. 387. Republished with permission of *The University of Chicago Law Review*, conveyed through Copyright Clearance Center and the author.

As you read, consider the following questions:

1. What large exceptions exist in the anticruelty provisions of state laws, according to Sunstein?

2. Under what conditions does Sunstein feel hunting should be banned?

3. Why does Sunstein feel that more people are not focused on reform of state law to protect animal rights?

There are nearly sixty million domestic dogs in the United States, owned by over thirty-six million households. Over half of these households give Christmas presents to their dogs. Millions of them celebrate their dog's birthday. If a family's dog were somehow forced to live a short and painful life, the family would undoubtedly feel some combination of rage and grief. What can be said about dog owners can also be said about cat owners, who are more numerous still. But through their daily behavior, people who love those pets, and greatly care about their welfare, help ensure short and painful lives for millions, even billions of animals that cannot easily be distinguished from dogs and cats. Should people change their behavior? Should the law promote animal welfare? Should animals have legal rights? To answer these questions, we need to step back a bit.

Past Views on Animal Rights

Many people think that the very idea of animal rights is implausible. Suggesting that animals are neither rational nor self-aware, [eighteenth-century German philosopher] Immanuel Kant thought of animals as "man's instruments," deserving protection only to help human beings in their relation to one another: "He who is cruel to animals becomes hard also in his dealings with men." [Eighteenth-century English philosopher and animal rights advocate] Jeremy Bentham took a different approach, suggesting that mistreatment of animals was akin to slavery and racial discrimination:

> The day *may* come, when the rest of the animal creation may acquire those rights which never could have been withholden from them but by the hand of tyranny. The French have already discovered that the blackness of the skin is no reason why a human being should be abandoned without redress to the caprice of a tormentor. . . . A full-grown horse or dog is beyond comparison a more rational, as well as a more conversable animal, than an infant of a day, or a week, or even month, old. But suppose the case were otherwise, what would it avail? the question is not, Can they *reason*? Nor, Can they *talk*? But, Can they *suffer*?

John Stuart Mill concurred, repeating the analogy to slavery.

Most people reject that analogy. But in the last ten years, the animal rights question has moved from the periphery and toward the center of political and legal debate. The debate is international. In 2002, Germany became the first European nation to vote to guarantee animal rights in its constitution, adding the words "and the animals" to a clause that obliges the state to respect and protect the dignity of human beings. The European Union has done a great deal to reduce animal suffering. Within the United States, consumer pressures have been leading to improved conditions for animals used as food. Notwithstanding its growing appeal, the idea of animal rights has been disputed with extraordinary intensity. Some advocates of animal rights think that their adversaries are selfish, unthinking, cruel, even morally blind. Some of those who oppose animal rights think that the advocates are fanatical and even bizarre, willing to trample on important human interests for the sake of rats and mice and salmon. . . .

Anticruelty Laws

The anticruelty provisions of state law contain extraordinarily large exceptions. They do not ban hunting, and generally they do not regulate hunting in a way that is designed to protect animals against suffering. Usually, they do not apply to the use of animals for medical or scientific purposes. To a large degree, they do not apply to the production and use of animals as food. The latter exemption is the most important. About ten billion animals are killed for food annually in the United States; indeed, 24,000,000 chickens and some 323,000 pigs are slaughtered every day. The cruel and abusive practices generally involved in contemporary farming are largely unregulated at the state level. Because the overwhelming majority of animals are produced and used for food, the coverage of anticruelty laws is exceedingly narrow. . . .

Increased Regulation

I think that we should go further. We should focus attention not only on the "enforcement gap," but also on the areas where current law offers little or no protection. In short, *the law should impose further regulation on hunting, scientific experiments, entertainment, and (above all) farming to ensure against unnecessary animal suffering.* It is easy to imagine a set of initiatives that would do a great deal here, and indeed European nations have moved in just this direction. There are many possibilities.

Federal law might, for example, require scientists to justify experiments on animals by showing, in front of some kind of committee or board, that (a) such experiments are actually necessary or promising and (b) the animals involved will be subjected to as little suffering as possible. Some steps have already been taken in this direction, but it would be reasonable to go much further. If dogs or chimpanzees are going to be used to explore some medical treatment, it should be necessary to ensure that they will be decently fed and housed. Similar controls might be imposed on agriculture. If cows, hens, and pigs are going to be raised for use as food, they should be treated decently in terms of nutrition, space requirements, and

The Welfare of All Animals

Why should we ground values in the welfare of human beings rather than in the welfare of all beings capable of having a welfare at all? That many nonhuman animals have interests and welfares is difficult to deny, for they are certainly capable of feeling pain and suffering as well as pleasure and joy. There is no nonreligious reason why the pains and pleasures of nonhuman animals should not be given equal weight with the similar pains and pleasures of human beings.

Peter Singer, "Taking Humanism Beyond Speciesism,"
Free Inquiry, *vol. 24, no. 6, October–November 2004, pp. 19–21.*

overall care. European nations have taken significant steps of this sort. The European Union [EU], for example, has decided to ban the standard bare wire cage for hens, and to require that they be provided with access to a perch and nesting box for laying eggs.

Decreased Suffering

If we focus on suffering, as I believe we should, it is not necessarily impermissible to kill animals and use them for food; but it is entirely impermissible to be indifferent to their interests while they are alive. So too for other animals in farms, even or perhaps especially if they are being used for the benefit of human beings. If sheep are going to be used to create clothing, their conditions should be conducive to their welfare. We might ban hunting altogether, at least if its sole purpose is human recreation. (Should animals be hunted and killed simply because people enjoy hunting and killing them? The issue would be different if hunting and killing could be justified as having important functions, such as control of populations, the search for food, or protection of human beings against animal violence.)

As a minimal reform step, it would even be possible to imagine a system in which companies disclosed their practices, either voluntarily or as part of a mandate. Companies that protected animals from suffering, and ensured decent conditions, might publicize that fact, and attempt to receive a market boost from the practices. Companies that treated animals cruelly, and were forced to disclose that fact, might well be punished by consumers.

I believe that steps in this direction would make a great deal of sense. But here things become far more controversial. Why is this? Partly it is because of sheer ignorance, on the part of most people, about what actually happens to animals in (for example) farming and scientific experimentation. I am confident that much greater regulation would be actively sought if current practices were widely known. Partly the controversy is a product of the political power of the relevant interests, which intensely resist regulation. But legitimate questions might be raised about these regulatory strategies for one simple reason: The legitimate interests of animals and the legitimate interests of human beings are in conflict in some of these areas. Here as elsewhere, additional regulation would be costly and burdensome. Regulation of scientific experiments on animals may lead to fewer experiments—and hence to less in the way of scientific and medical progress. If farms are regulated, the price of meat will increase, and people will be able to eat less meat. Hence it is necessary to weigh the gain to animal welfare against the harms to human beings. If the health of human beings could be seriously compromised by regulation of experiments on animals and farming, there is reason to engage in some balancing before supporting that regulation.

Analyzing Values

Any such balancing must depend, in part, on values—on how much weight we should assign to the relevant interests. At the very least, I suggest that suffering and harm to animals should count, and that any measures that impose suffering and harm should be convincingly justified. The mere hedonic gain provided by improved cosmetics and perfume does not seem sufficient to justify the infliction of real suffering. Eating beef might well fall into the same category. To make a sensible assessment, it would be helpful to know a great deal about the facts, not only about values. One of the most important disputes in the domain of scientific experimentation is whether and to what extent the relevant experiments really hold out a great deal of promise for medical progress. If we are speaking of perfumes, the claim for imposing suffering on animals is ludicrously weak. But if scientists are able to develop treatments for AIDS and cancer, or even treatment for serious psychological ailments, the claim is much stronger.

Now some animal rights advocates might urge that even if the gains from a certain practice are very large, experiments are not justified. We do not, after all, allow scientists to experiment on human beings, even human beings with serious disabilities, when and because medical advances would be significant. Indeed, scientists are not permitted to experiment on human beings who are incapable of consciousness, or of suffering, because of some permanent incapacitation. Should research be permitted on such people? If not, a simple answer would be that the research would be intolerable to friends and family members. But what if the research would have great benefits? Should any balancing be permitted? And what if some of those who are permanently incapacitated lack friends and family members?

It is not so clear, in my view, that an assessment of social consequences, and of possible benefits, is irrelevant to the judgment whether to allow medical experiments in such circumstances. Perhaps the firm moral prohibition is best supported by the suggestion that any power to experiment on permanently incapacitated human beings would be hard to limit in practice, and that we do better, all things considered, never to investigate consequences in particular cases. It seems to me difficult to justify a similar prohibition on any experimentation on nonhuman animals. I believe that it would be excessive to ban experiments that impose a degree of suffering on rats or mice if the consequence of those experiments would be to produce significant medical advances for human beings (and ultimately nonhuman animals as well). . . .

Every reasonable person believes in animal rights. Even the sharpest critics of animal rights support the anticruelty laws. I have suggested that the simple moral judgment behind these laws is that animal suffering matters. This judgment supports a significant amount of reform. Most modestly, private suits should be permitted to prevent illegal cruelty and neglect. There is no good reason to give public officials a monopoly on enforcement; that monopoly is a recipe for continued illegality. Less modestly, anticruelty laws should be extended to areas that are now exempt from them, including scientific experiments and farming. There is no good reason to permit the level of suffering that is now being experienced by millions, even billions of living creatures.

> *"Life in the suburbs has become a war*
> *of attrition, and Bambi and his mom*
> *are winning."*

When Done Ethically, Hunting Can Be Humane

Mary Zeiss Stange

In this viewpoint, Mary Zeiss Stange discusses the approaches different suburban and urban developments are taking to address the nuisance deer issue. She notes that solutions such as sterilization and relocation have proved ineffective and that some communities have hired sharpshooters to thin the herd. Stange advocates the use of highly regulated skilled local hunters to decrease deer numbers humanely, economically, and effectively. Mary Zeiss Stange is an author and a professor at Skidmore College in New York.

As you read, consider the following questions:

1. According to Stange, why is contraception ineffective in controlling deer numbers in many communities?

2. What are the methods that Stange states are used by companies hired to thin deer herds?

Mary Zeiss Stange, "Why Deer Hunts Can Be Humane," *USA Today*, December 20, 2005, p. 13A. Reproduced by permission of the author.

3. According to Stange, why are urban hunts more humane and ethical than a team of sharpshooters?

At first, they are charming visitors. Sylph-like, whitetail deer amble into the backyard, cropping a dandelion here and a bit of clover there. Startled by your appearance on the deck, they gracefully bound over the fence. Thrilled, you feel fortunate to live this close to nature.

Years pass and these same adorable mega-faunas, growing in numbers and audacity, have taken on the aura of a plague. They trash flower beds, decimate vegetable gardens, denude deciduous trees and shrubs. Far from dashing away, they train those liquid brown eyes on you with a look you have come to associate with a cervid version of zombies. Life in the suburbs has become a war of attrition, and Bambi and his mom are winning.

It's a story being played out across the USA, in many major metropolitan areas. Deer are, by nature, browsers—they eat a broad range of fruits, flowers, grasses and greenery. Add to this the fact that they are highly adaptable, and the convergence of whitetail and humans' taste in landscaping is bound to become a problem.

Encroachment

To be fair, it probably started when the first homesteader who planted a garden wound up cussing the deer who helped themselves to the first pickings. The problem is becoming exacerbated by the suburban and ex-urban developments that are vastly encroaching upon whitetail habitat. Make no mistake: The deer are not "wandering into" these sprawling developments. They were there first. And, at this point, they have nowhere else to go.

Take the case of Ramsey County, Minn. In the Highwood neighborhood in St. Paul and South Maplewood to the east, according to St. Paul City Councilmember Kathy Lantry, deer are so numerous "they've become like rats," and so destructive that one former resident remarked, "You can't plant anything. They eat it all."

How to solve the problem? Hunting the rural fringes of the development has not sufficiently reduced whitetail numbers. Relocation doesn't work: It is costly and labor-intensive, many deer don't survive it, and the ones that do often simply become somebody else's headache.

Contraception is an option, although it too is expensive, and generally unreliable. Wildlife management officials in Princeton Township, N.J., were hopeful that they had turned the corner on their perennial deer problem last year, when they injected more than 50 does with [the contraceptive vaccine] SpayVac. Come springtime, with two dozen spotted fawns prancing about Princeton's avenues, they declared the experiment a "disappointment." Some pilot studies, in places as far-flung as Houston and the New Jersey suburbs, have suggested somewhat more promise. But significant problems remain: What, for example, are the implications—ethical as well as ecological—of manipulating the gene pool?

Will the fact that inoculated does go into heat multiple times place impossible stress on the buck population, as well as precipitating even more deer-vehicle accidents? And there is the bottom line: Deer can live up to 15 years, so even successfully sterilized ones will be munching on the hollyhocks, and darting in and out of traffic, for the foreseeable future.

Ramsey County, along with a growing number of other municipalities, has decided to call in the heavy artillery, in the form of a team of sharpshooters to thin 200 does from the herd.

Tony DeNicola and his crew from White Buffalo Inc., a non-profit corporation based in Connecticut, are pros. In a relatively straightforward situation such as St. Paul, where whitetails tend to congregate in park areas, they shoot deer over bait with high-powered rifles from vehicles and tree stands. Fees range from $200–$350 per deer, depending on the project's difficulty. "I do this every day," DeNicola has said. "For me, it's like brushing my teeth."

In some less open spaces, White Buffalo opts for the "capture-and-kill" method, in which baited deer are trapped in nets and killed with a metal bolt administered at point blank range to the head. It's the same device used in slaughterhouses.

Appalling Approach

One need not be an animal rights activist to be appalled by this way of dealing with "nuisance deer." Indeed, hunters have been among the most vocal critics. Neighboring hunters offered to help thin the herd at no taxpayer expense, but John Moriarty, Ramsey County's natural resource manager overseeing the cull in St. Paul and South Maplewood, rebuffed them: "There's no way you can have people with guns shooting deer in the city."

But, actually, you can. All that skilled hunters need to do the job are access and homeowners' permission, and several metropolitan areas that have established "urban hunts" do provide both—among them are Cincinnati, Pittsburgh, Philadelphia, Chicago, Detroit, and some counties around the Twin Cities [Minneapolis/St. Paul].

Though most of these urban hunts involve archery rather than firearms, all have three things in common: They are highly regulated, and only very well-qualified hunters make the cut. As a result, they are very safe; there are no documented cases of injuries to *non-hunters* in any urban deer hunts. And they do work to bring down deer numbers—perhaps not quite so dramatically as a sharpshooting fest, but certainly more humanely, economically and ethically. The meat from these urban hunts generally goes to community food banks.

There is an additional advantage to urban hunts: It reminds the deer, and us, about our respective places in the scheme of things.

Urban hunts can help make deer more wary of coming into contact with human beings. They also remind the people that they are more than mere sightseers in the neighborhoods they and the deer both now call home.

| "It is right to exploit nature to promote
| our own lives and happiness."

Humans Ought to Use Nature to Serve Their Own Needs

Tibor R. Machan

In the following selection, Tibor R. Machan discusses the weak case for animal rights and suggests that the human right to utilize natural resources is greater than any animal's rights. Machan supports this position through examples of wildlife brutality. He notes the lack of logic in the concept of animal rights and emphasizes the difference between humans and animals. Machan is an author, a columnist, a professor emeritus of philosophy at Auburn University in Alabama, and the R.C. Hoiles Chair of Business Ethics and Free Enterprise at the Argyros School of Business and Economics at Chapman University in California.

As you read, consider the following questions:

1. According to Machan, what is the major difference between human and animal rights?
2. What concept governs the behavior of animals in the wild, in Machan's view?

3. What does Machan say animals must possess before they can be given rights?

Not long ago, a television talk show featured several animal rights advocates who enjoyed considerable airtime to defend their position both analytically and emotionally.

The program exhibited little of that famous media virtue: "balance." Almost everyone, including the host, championed the animal rights position. A law professor was on hand to raise a few skeptical questions, yet even this guest provided no clear-cut argument against the idea that animals enjoy rights akin to those of human beings.

One legal specialist claimed that animals must be regarded as possessing the exact same right to freedom that we assign to individual human beings. We heard how this guest had offered shelter to six dogs and were then told that this is a model that ought to be emulated throughout the world. The act was characterized as constituting a grant of asylum to the dogs—just as one might grant asylum to a political refugee from a totalitarian society.

This is also the position held by Harvard law professor Steve Wise, who has been making the rounds advocating full legal protection for at least "higher" animals like the great apes. Wise even claims to believe that these animals possess a moral nature—which, if true, would certainly give his case a fairly solid foundation inasmuch as rights are the political–legal instruments by which the moral nature of human beings is afforded scope and protection.

The Real Animal Kingdom

When the show was over, I merely filed away the experience, having already dealt with the issue of animal rights in many and various places. But then along came a *National Geographic Explorer* program on CNBC that in great detail depicted a polar bear's hunt for baby seals. First, we saw how the bear managed to capture and kill a baby seal. Next, we saw a mature polar bear fending off a young polar bear intent on the same seal carcass.

And then the narrator said something that was very interesting: "The older males are known to kill younger ones when fighting over carcasses."

The observation brought to mind the animal rights program of the night before and all its pat assumptions. How inconvenient that wild animals do not always behave with scrupulous decorum! No, the older bears do not share even a bit of the scavenged pickings but rather chase the young ones away or kill them outright, the better to keep everything for themselves. These greedy, violent animals seemed oblivious to the legal–moral status that had been conferred on them by the animal rights panelists just a few nights before. (Well, perhaps they don't get cable.)

Human Values

Of course, human beings have slugged it out over scarce resources throughout history (although in more recent times, as the values of civilization have taken stronger root, the win-win approach of the humane economy has tended to displace the dog-eat-dog approach of violence and warfare). But in most eras and in most places, it has always been a crime to kill a young person even in defense of one's property, let alone over wild prey. And where it isn't a crime, the bulk of world opinion regards such societies as barbaric and brutal, even in this age of multiculturalism.

So, given the evident lack of moral sense of even the highest rungs in the animal world, how can we seriously entertain the idea that animals have rights like human beings do? If such rights and such moral sensibility could be imputed to them, all the brutality in the animal world would have to be construed as criminal. But, quite sensibly, it is not. Why not?

Animals Are Property

We have quite enough difficulty in persuading or coercing human beings to respect the rights of their fellows, so that all can live in peace. By treating animals as our moral equals, we would undermine the liberty and dignity of human beings—making the slaughters of [Adolf] Hitler, [Joseph] Stalin, or Pol Pot seem no worse than the daily activity of preparing cattle for market. That is one kind of moral equivalence we must never allow. Animals are properly property. To misunderstand the rights of animals is to cheapen the rights of human beings.

Richard A. Epstein, "The Next Rights Revolution?: *It's Bowser's Time at Last—Examination and Refutation of Animal* *Rights Activists' Arguments,"* National Review, *November 8, 1999.*

Animals and Instinct

The reason is that animals, as a rule, behave as instinct dictates. In many cases, instincts dictate that the animals kill their own kind. Fish often eat their young, as do lions when impelled to do so by their genetic disposition, presumably to rid their pride of bastard offspring. Animals have no choice about how they conduct themselves, so no one can reasonably issue indictments against them, moral or legal (a practice once in force throughout Christian Europe, however). Inborn, hardwired prompters govern their lives.

On an intuitive level, everyone understands this, even the advocates of animal rights. Yes, some scientists argue that perhaps some of the higher animals, such as great apes or orangutans, have actually developed "culture," but this conclusion is based more on wishful—anthropomorphic—interpretation than any real evidence of culture and thought.

On the other hand, when people act brutally, we do feel justified in condemning them. Why? Why is it regarded as barbaric—and why should it be criminal—to kill children for fun, profit, or even survival if the lower animals can't rightly be blamed for violent behavior? Why indeed implore us to treat animals more humanely than some of us do?

I argue that what warrants such evaluation of human beings is that we are in fact fundamentally different from our animal kin in the wild.

Human Morality

The issues at stake are neither trivial nor academic, for they speak directly to the moral standing of human beings on this earth and how we should live our lives during the brief time we're here—whether we should be enjoying ourselves as best we can, or lashing ourselves continuously with a cat-o'-nine-tails in penitence for all the ants we stepped on today.

Sadly, environmentalists—not all of them, but all too many—seem to despise human beings and what we have wrought on this earth. They loathe all the invented, artificial, "unnatural" joys that spring from human imagination and human industry. From bridges to trains and planes to coal mines and soot-producing factories, it's all a dastardly affront, a rape of nature, in their eyes. A few—a very few, we must hope—would just as soon see humans out of the picture. The ... sentiment of environmentalist David Graber, who hopes for the "right virus" to come along and decimate humanity, suggests that at least some radical environmentalists must be unhappy that medical researchers have killed a few monkeys in their search for the cause of the enigmatic SARS (severe acute respiratory syndrome) virus. Here we have a potentially dual affront: Animals have been killed, and humans might be saved.

It is indisputable that human activity sometimes causes environmental and other problems that must be dealt with.

But it is one thing to argue for viable solutions to these problems. It is quite another to argue that humankind must leave the earth untouched altogether! I, for one, am grateful for all the despoiling. I don't want to do without air travel, word processing, or the Internet. I would have no fun—indeed, hardly any life—at all in a state of nature living off nuts and berries.

It is right for human beings to indulge in distinctively human activities. It is right to exploit nature to promote our own lives and happiness. There is no reason to feel guilt or shame about it.

We are very much a part of nature—and nature is very much a part of us, too. [I argue] that no animals possess rights unless they also possess a moral nature—a capacity for discerning between right and wrong and choosing between alternatives. It is this moral capacity that establishes a basis for rights, not the fact that animals, like us, have interests or can feel pain.

This [essay] does not make a pitch for specific public policy changes but instead explores the standards of environmental philosophy on which public policy about the environment must rest. Central to this philosophy is the view that human beings are of paramount importance when public policies and, indeed, standards of personal conduct vis-à-vis the environment are being established. Whether it is possible to direct public policy toward an environmentalism that accepts humans as first in the hierarchy of nature depends on many factors, including what people believe about the place of human beings in the natural world. It also depends on whether a sound environmentalism can be crafted when humans are indeed put first. [I propose] that the answer is yes—indeed, that a human-first environmentalism is the only kind of environmentalism worth having.

Periodical Bibliography

The following articles have been selected to supplement the diverse views presented in this chapter.

Jim Amrhein
"No Inherent Animal Rights: 'Righting' a Wrong," *Whiskey and Gunpowder*, March 28, 2005. www.whiskeyandgunpowder.com.

Richard Brookhiser
"Straight Shooting," *National Review*, November 20, 2006.

Tom Dickson
"Hunting Myths: Dispelling Some Myths About Hunting," Minnesota Department of Natural Resources, 2007. www.dnr.state.mn.us/hunting/tips/myths.html.

Kathy Etling
"Animal Activists Want Your Children," *The American Hunter*, February 2007.

Camilla Fox
"The Case Against Sport Hunting," *Animal Issues*, Summer 2002.

Gary L. Francione
"Our Hypocrisy," *New Scientists*, June 4, 2005.

Graham Harvey
"Hunting Animals Is Wrong," *Open Democracy.net*, December 13, 2002. www.openDemocracy.net.

Edwin Locke
"Animal 'rights' Versus Human Rights," *Intellectual Conservatives.com*, June 2, 2005, www.intellectualconservative.com.

Dean Peerman
"Unsportsmanlike Conduct," *The Christian Century*, March 6, 2007.

Michael Tichelar
"Putting Animals into Politics," *Rural History*, October 6, 2006.

Steve Tuttle
"The Elusive Hunter," *Newsweek*, April 12, 2006.

For Further Discussion

Chapter 1

1. Ward M. Clark, Mark Rowlands, and Gary Yourofsky present differing moral perspectives on the ethics of hunting. Which author makes the strongest fact-based case for his position? Which author makes the strongest emotional argument?

2. Mark Rowlands states that hunting is only acceptable when necessary for human survival. Using the discussion and guidelines from his article, can you think of any other situations beyond those he specifically describes in which Rowlands might feel hunting would also be acceptable? Do you believe Gary Yourofsky would accept hunting in these situations? Please explain your answer.

3. After reading Heidi Prescott's and Brian Donlon's arguments for and against teaching children to hunt, do you feel that acquisition of the skills that Donlon describes are worth the risks Prescott describes? Please support your opinion using information from the articles.

Chapter 2

1. Based on your consideration of the viewpoints of Jim Zumbo and Jim Carmichel, do you think that it is more ethical to learn hunting using the new technological innovations, or do you think standard hunting procedures are equally ethical or more ethical than technology-assisted hunting? Why or why not?

2. Jim Carmichel states that technological innovations have negatively impacted hunting. Do you think he would agree that his arguments could be a critique of modern

society's reliance on technological shortcuts? Use examples from the viewpoint to support your opinion.

3. When Internet hunting emerged as a reality, the animal rights movement decried the practice as the worst form of canned hunting. After reading the articles by Steven Christian and the Humane Society of the United States, do you agree? Do you think there is another form of canned hunting that could be considered worse by animal rights activists? Explain.

Chapter 3

1. In Yong Chau's interview, Anne Muller states that wildlife managers intentionally manipulate habitat and wildlife populations in a manner that is destructive to the environment, ecology, biology, and even certain businesses. Do you think that her argument in support of this assertion is stronger than those of Sharon Levy and Hal Herring? Why or why not?

2. What solutions do Sharon Levy and Hal Herring suggest for preserving forests? Evaluate the possible effectiveness and drawbacks of the solutions. How does your critique of their solutions differ from Anne Muller's critique in Yong Chau's interview?

3. In her article, Jane Goodall calls for an international solution to the problem of decreasing species. Do you feel that Bob Holmes's suggestion to intertwine trophy hunting with conservation could be considered an adequate response to Goodall's challenge? Explain your answer with detailed examples from the viewpoints.

Chapter 4

1. In its viewpoint, People for the Ethical Treatment of Animals (PETA) states that hunting is cruel and inhumane because many animals suffer prolonged, painful deaths

when they are injured but not killed by hunters. Mike Lapierre asserts in his viewpoint that hunters are highly motivated to kill on the first shot. If a weapon were to be developed that could kill an animal on the first shot every time, do you think that hunters would use it? Do you think PETA would support its use? Explain.

2. Mary Zeiss Stange asserts that highly regulated urban deer hunts involving skilled archers is more humane than shooting deer with high-powered rifles from vehicles and tree stands. Do you agree with this assertion? Do you feel that one form of hunting is more ethical than the other?

3. Cass Sunstein contends that animals have a moral claim to protection from harm and laws regulating hunting should be stiffened to protect this right. How does Tibor R. Machan respond to this argument and suggestion? Which viewpoint is more convincing and why?

Organizations to Contact

The editors have compiled the following list of organizations concerned with the issues debated in this book. The descriptions are derived from materials provided by the organizations. All have publications or information available for interested readers. The list was compiled on the date of publication of the present volume; the information provided here may change. Be aware that many organizations take several weeks or longer to respond to inquiries, so allow as much time as possible.

American Forests
PO Box 2000, Washington, DC   20013
(202) 955-4500
Web site: www.americanforests.org

American Forests is the nation's oldest nonprofit citizens' conservation organization and a world leader in planting trees for environmental restoration, a pioneer in the science and practice of urban forestry, and a primary communicator of the benefits of trees and forests. The organization believes that hunting and fishing under proper regulation are important tools in the management of a healthy forest ecosystem. American Forests publishes a monthly e-mail newsletter called *Forest-Bytes* and a quarterly magazine, *American Forests*.

American Humane Association
63 Inverness Dr. East, Englewood, CO   80112-5117
(800) 227-4645
Web site: www.americanhumane.org

The American Humane Association is a national organization dedicated to protecting both children and animals. The association assists in developing policies, legislation, curricula, and training programs to protect children and animals from cruelty, abuse, neglect, and exploitation. The organization is opposed to the hunting of any living creature for fun, for a trophy, or for sport. Fact sheets and legislative briefs dealing with current issues related to the protection of children and animals are available on its Web site.

Ducks Unlimited, Inc. (DU)
One Waterfowl Way, Memphis, TN   38120
(901) 758-3825
Web site: www.ducksunlimited.org

Ducks Unlimited (DU) conserves, restores, and manages wetlands and associated habitats for North America's waterfowl. The group values and enjoys the sport and heritage of hunting. The DU publishes the bimonthly *DU Magazine*, a paper newsletter, and an electronic newsletter. The organization also produces TV and radio programs.

Friends of Animals, Inc. (FoA)
777 Post Rd.. Suite 205, Darien, CT   06820
(203) 656-1522
Web site: www.friendsofanimals.org

Friends of Animals (FoA) is a nonprofit, international animal-advocacy organization that works to cultivate a respectful view of nonhuman animals, free-living and domestic. The FoA's goal is to free animals from cruelty and institutionalized exploitation around the world. FoA feels that hunting is cruel, deceitful, socially unjustifiable, and ecologically disruptive. The organization publishes books, booklets, and brochures on topics ranging from hunting to vegetarian cooking.

Humane Society Legislative Fund (HSLF)
519 C St. NE, Washington, DC   20002
(202) 676-2314
Web site: www.fund.org

The Humane Society Legislative Fund (HSLF) is a social welfare organization that supports animal protection laws at the state and federal level, educates the public about animal protection issues, and promotes humane candidates for office.

HSLF is opposed to the recreational killing of wildlife and is a separate lobbying affiliate of the Humane Society of the United States. HSLF publishes the *Humane Scorecard*, which tracks the voting records of members of Congress, as well as a voter guide, which makes recommendations for supporting humane candidates.

Humane Society of the United States (HSUS)
2100 L St. NW, Washington, DC   20037
(202) 452-1100
Web site: www.hsus.org

The Humane Society of the United States (HSUS) promotes the protection of all animals by celebrating the human-animal bond and fighting animal cruelty and abuse in all of its forms. HSUS strongly opposes the hunting of any living creature for fun, trophy, or sport because of the trauma, suffering, and death that result. The organization does, however, recognize that the legitimate needs for human subsistence and the welfare and management of animals may on occasion necessitate the killing of wildlife. The Humane Society Press publishes books focusing on subjects of particular interest to policy makers, academics, and professionals working in the field of animal care and welfare.

Izaak Walton League of America (IWLA)
707 Conservation Ln., Gaithersburg, MD   20878
(301) 548-0150
Web site: www.iwla.org

The Izaak Walton League of America (IWLA) is a conservation organization created to defend wild America by changing public policy. The organization is dedicated to "protecting our country's natural heritage and improving outdoor recreation opportunities for all Americans." It believes that hunting should be considered a valuable management tool when it is compatible with other resources, uses, and purposes. Its publications include a newsletter, a magazine, and various issue-based policy reports.

National Rifle Association of America (NRA)
11250 Waples Mill Rd., Fairfax, VA 22030
(800) 672-3888
Web site: www.nra.org

The National Rifle Association of America (NRA) was founded to promote firearms education. It has continued its mandate of firearms education, but is also a major political lobby to defend the Constitution's Second Amendment right to bear arms. The NRA strongly supports every law-abiding American's privilege to hunt. Its publications include *American Rifleman, American Hunter, Shooting Illustrated, Shooting Sports USA, NRA Insights,* and *America's First Freedom.*

National Shooting Sports Foundation (NSSF)
11 Mile Hill Rd., Newtown, CT 06470-2359
(203) 426-1320
Web site: www.nssf.org

The National Shooting Sports Foundation (NSSF) is the trade association for the shooting, hunting, and firearms industry. The group focuses on measurably advancing participation in and understanding of hunting and the shooting sports, reaffirming and strengthening its members' commitment to the safe and responsible use of firearms, and promoting a political climate supportive of America's traditional firearms rights. The NSSF has developed a variety of safety and conservation publications and videos.

National Wildlife Federation (NWF)
11100 Wildlife Center Dr., Reston, VA 20190
(703) 438-6000
Web site: www.nwf.org

The National Wildlife Federation's (NWF's) goal is to inspire Americans to protect wildlife for future generations. The NWF supports conservation efforts and hunting, under professional regulation. The NWF publishes several magazines, including *Ranger Rick, Your Big Backyard, Wild Animal Baby,* and *National Wildlife.*

People for the Ethical Treatment of Animals (PETA)
501 Front St., Norfolk, VA   23510
(757) 622-7382
Web site: www.peta.org

People for the Ethical Treatment of Animals (PETA) is the largest animal rights organization in the world. PETA advocates for animals through public education, cruelty investigations, research, animal rescue, legislation, special events, celebrity involvement, and protest campaigns. PETA believes that hunting is cruel and unnecessary. PETA's literature includes articles, pamphlets, books, and magazines.

United States Sportsmen's Alliance
801 Kingsmill Pkwy., Columbus, OH   43229
(614) 888-4868
Web site: www.ussportsmen.org

The United States Sportsmen's Alliance provides direct lobbying and grassroots coalition support to protect and advance the rights of hunters, fishermen, trappers, and scientific wildlife management professionals through coalition building, ballot issue campaigning, and legislative and government relations. The U.S. Sportsmen's Alliance believes that regulated hunting, fishing, and trapping are wholesome experiences and reliable wildlife-management tools. Its publications include quarterly magazines, a newsletter, and fact sheets about hunting, fishing, and trapping.

Wilderness Society
1615 M St. NW, Washington, DC   20036
(800) 843-9453
Web site: www.wilderness.org

The Wilderness Society is a conservation organization that brings together scientific expertise, analysis, and bold advocacy to save, protect, and restore America's wilderness areas. The organization views hunting as a legitimate use in wilderness areas, national forests, and certain wildlife areas subject to appropriate regulation for species protection. The Wilderness Society publishes a quarterly newsletter and an annual magazine.

Wildlife Management Institute (WMI)

1146 19th St. NW, Suite 700, Washington, DC 20036
(202) 371-1808
Web site: www.wildlifemanagementinstitute.com

The Wildlife Management Institute (WMI) is a professional conservation organization that works to improve the professional foundation of wildlife management. The institute supports and encourages recreational hunting that is conducted legally, safely, and ethically.

The Wildlife Society (TWS)

5410 Governor Ln., Suite 200, Bethesda, MD 20814-2144
(301) 897-9770
Web site: www.wildlife.org

The Wildlife Society (TWS) is a scientific and educational association dedicated to excellence in wildlife stewardship through science and education. The society feels that hunting, when based on biological information and properly regulated, can be used effectively to responsibly manage wildlife populations. TWS publishes a quarterly magazine.

World Wildlife Fund (WWF)

1250 Twenty-Fourth St. NW, Washington, DC 20037-1132
(202) 293-4800
Web site: www.worldwildlife.org

The World Wildlife Fund (WWF) is dedicated to protecting rare and endangered species and habitats all over the world. The organization explicitly objects to any activity that threatens either the survival of a species or the conservation of wilderness areas that support the species. It does not, however, oppose hunting by indigenous peoples for basic food and shelter needs. The WWF publishes its research in scientific journals and books, produces management plans and conservation strategies used in the field, and contributes proposals and recommendations to policy debates.

Bibliography of Books

William M. Adams	*Against Extinction: The Story of Conservation*, London: Earthscan, 2004.
Priscilla Cohn	*Ethics and Wildlife*, Lewiston, NY: Edwin Mellen, 1999.
David Degrazia	*Animal Rights: A Very Short Introduction*, Oxford: Oxford University Press, 2002.
Jan Dizard	*Mortal Stakes: Hunters and Hunting in Contemporary America*, Amherst: University of Massachusetts Press, 2003.
Randall Eaton	*The Sacred Hunt*, Ashland, OR: Sacred Press, 1999.
Terry Grosz	*No Safe Refuge: Man as Predator in the World of Wildlife*, Boulder, CO: Johnson, 2003.
Arthur Jaggard	*The Ethics of Bow Hunting for Deer*, Bloomington, IN: Authorhouse, 2004.
David Petersen	*Heartsblood: Hunting, Spirituality, and Wildness in America*, Boulder, CO: Johnson, 2003.
Jim Posewitz	*Inherit the Hunt*, Guilford, CT: Globe Pequot, 2001.
Tom Regan	*The Case for Animal Rights*, Berkeley: University of California Press, 2004.

Philip Rowter — *The Hunting Instinct: Safari Chronicles on Hunting Game, Conservation, and Management in the Republic of South Africa and Namibia 1990–1998*, Huntington Beach, CA: Safari, 2nd ed., 2006.

David E. Samuel — *Know Hunting: Truth, Lies, and Myths*, Cheat Lake, WV: Know Hunting, 1999.

Peter Singer and Jim Mason — *The Ethics of What We Eat: Why Our Food Choices Matter*, New York: Rodale, 2007.

Cass Sunstein — *Animal Rights: Current Debates and New Directions*, New York: Oxford University Press, 2005.

James A. Swan — *The Sacred Art of Hunting: Myths, Legends, and the Modern Mythos*, Minocqua WI: Willow Creek, 2000.

Angus Taylor — *Animals and Ethics*, Peterborough, ON: Broadview, 2003.

The Animal Studies Group — *Killing Animals*, Urbana: University of Illinois Press, 2006.

Gary E. Varner — *In Nature's Interests?: Interests, Animal Rights, and Environmental Ethics*, New York: Oxford University Press, 2002.

Steven M. Wise — *Rattling the Cage: Toward Legal Rights for Animals*, Cambridge, MA: Perseus, 2000.

Index